A Fast Ride Out
of Here

A Fast Ride Out of Here

Confessions of Rock's Most Dangerous Man

Pete Way

With Paul Rees

Constable • London

CONSTABLE

First published in Great Britain in 2017 by Constable

1 3 5 7 9 10 8 6 4 2

A CIP catalogue record for this book
is available from the British Library.

ISBN 978-1-47212-431-9 (hardback)
ISBN 978-1-47212-432-6 (trade paperback)

Typeset in Bembo by SX Composing DTP, Rayleigh, Essex
Printed and bound in Great Britain by Clays Ltd, St Ives plc

Papers used by Constable are from well-managed forests
and other responsible sources.

Constable
An imprint of
Little, Brown Book Group
Carmelite House
50 Victoria Embankment
London EC4Y 0DZ

An Hachette UK Company
www.hachette.co.uk

www.littlebrown.co.uk

This book is dedicated to the memory of Bethina and Joanna.
They will always live on in my heart.
P.W.

This one's to the memory of Nick Rogers,
who went with me to see UFO at
Birmingham Odeon in 1982.
P.R.

CONTENTS

'I remember seeing UFO in 1979 and one of the most memorable things about the concert was Pete Way's performance. He was one of the most charismatic bass players I had ever seen, and he has remained a uniquely individual player and performer to me from then on.'

Slash, Guns N' Roses – Los Angeles, May 2016

FOREWORD

As a teenager I was a huge UFO fan, so had obviously heard of Pete Way a good while before actually getting to meet him. I used to go and see them playing in and around London all the time. The first occasion was at the old Marquee Club on Wardour Street. I'm guessing that it would have been in 1974, because Michael Schenker was playing guitar with the band by then. I remember walking into the club that night and seeing Pete and UFO's singer, Phil Mogg, stood together at the bar. This was right before the gig. I didn't have the bottle to go up and talk to either of them, but just the fact of them being there seemed to me to be so cool.

Personally speaking, Pete's right up there at the top of the list of people who've inspired me. The most important thing for any band is the songs and his and UFO's were fantastic. Pete's a bloody good player and also underrated. If you try to play along to any of those songs that he's written, they've all got great bass lines and are really well structured. But I also loved Pete for his persona on stage. He was brilliant to watch and, for sure, some of that rubbed off on me and on all of us in Maiden. Pete had a style and stage presence like no one else and his influence is still there with me to this day.

It was a few years after that Marquee show that the photographer Ross Halfin introduced me to Pete. I had gone up to the Midlands to see UFO play at the Birmingham Odeon. Pete was brilliant to me. He took care of me, paid for my hotel room and made me feel really comfortable. He's such a nice guy and I've never forgotten that. Down the years I've done my best to try and look out for Pete whenever I can. I felt like I wanted to pay back a debt to him.

Maiden did a couple of gigs with UFO in California in the 1980s. They were the archetypal rock-and-roll rebels and pretty much excess all areas. Pete did a couple of shots of something or other before going on stage for the first show at Long Beach Arena. He told me that it steadied his nerves. Bloody hell, I'd have been all over the place with what he put away, but he went out and played perfectly well. What worked for Pete might not be a good idea for others. Certainly, I couldn't have got away with anything like what he did.

There isn't one particular favourite memory of being with Pete that I could pick out, because there are just so many of them. I remember hanging out with him at the Sunset Marquis hotel in Los Angeles and it just being mind-boggling to see him in action. Really, I still can't quite believe what Pete would get up to. But it was what everyone would expect a true rock and roller to do, so totally over the top. Everyone who has got to know Pete over the years will appreciate exactly what I'm talking about.

In reality, Pete's a bit of a Jekyll and Hyde character. You meet him and he's very quiet and a gentleman, and yet at the same time he would do and take any substance. It's almost as if there's two or even three people in there, but the one I know best is very easy-going and genuinely sweet-natured. Underneath it all I think Pete's quite shy, which I can relate to because I am too. Funnily enough, it was being around Pete that taught me to go in the opposite direction. Whereas he would do all kinds of everything to cover his shyness up, I didn't really go down that road. I tried a couple of times with booze, but I would be ill for three days. Pete can handle a hangover like no one else I know.

It would be true to say that Pete has been responsible for a lot of chaos, but who are we to pass judgement on him, or to say what he should or shouldn't have done? He's led a fantastic rock-and-roll life and totally lived it to the full. Ultimately, his legacy will be all those brilliant songs, his great showmanship and the fact that he's a lovely human being. And now I can't wait to read this book, especially to find out about all of the other stuff he's got up to that I didn't know about.

Steve Harris, Iron Maiden – Edmonton, Canada, April 2016

PROLOGUE

It's the year 1976 and out on the sun-baked West Coast of America, a young man with a song in his heart and a girl on his arm is living the rock-and-roll dream.

———

As I recall, 1 May 1976 was a typically warm, sunny California day and we left our hotel in a fleet of stretch black limousines. We drove out from the centre of San Francisco, over the Oakland Bridge and across the Bay, towards the Coliseum, which was where the local baseball team, the Oakland Raiders, played all of their home games. It was only a twenty-mile drive but it took hours in heavy traffic, slowed to a crawl because of the mass of people flocking to the stadium. It reminded me of being a kid back home in England and going for a drive to the seaside with Mum and Dad on a Bank Holiday weekend. We'd get stuck for hours in traffic jams, and looking back now it is as if my kid brother Neill and I spent the whole time either moaning or else fighting each other in the back of Dad's car.

I didn't mind the delay on this occasion; it could have taken us all day to get to the Coliseum for all that I cared. Right then, I was living out every rock-and-roll dream I'd ever had growing up as a teenager in Enfield, north London, and each day for me was like a new adventure. I was twenty-four years old and my band UFO's records seemed to be playing on American radio all of the time, especially out on the West Coast. We had toured the States pretty much non-stop for the past two years, and I had countless beautiful girls throw themselves at me and a friendly drug dealer in every major city. And now, our reward for all the hard work that we had put in was to play in front of 55,000 people at the Coliseum. To think, we even got paid for it! The money, the girls, the fast cars – none of that mattered next to being able to do a show like that; just the thought of it still makes the hairs stand up on the back of my neck.

In those days, the legendary Bill Graham promoted all of the outdoor shows at the Coliseum under the headline banner of Day on the Green. Bill had begun this series of events back in 1973 and, since then, everyone from Led Zeppelin and The Band to the Grateful Dead and Crosby, Stills, Nash & Young had done the Coliseum. Now, Bill had a reputation for being a tough customer. After all, he had been born Jewish in pre-war Berlin and was orphaned by the Nazis, but had escaped to France and then America. Bill wasn't a big guy and was quite softly-spoken, but he was passionate and imposing and you certainly wouldn't have wanted to cross him. He knew how to run a show, though, and while it was said that he wouldn't ever pay top dollar, he catered for musicians and was always very decent to us. The following year, we did another show for Bill at his Winterland Ballroom in San Francisco with the

Canadian band, Rush. We stormed the place that night – the crowd was still chanting for an encore when Rush's crew put the house lights back up. We didn't mind because Rush ran everything to a tight schedule, but there was almost a riot and Bill made a point of coming to see us in our dressing room. He told us that Rush should have let us play on and handed over an extra $2,000 to our tour manager, John Knowles. 'Guys,' he told us, 'that was great; now go and enjoy yourselves', and we never needed much encouragement in that respect. Ever after, Bill would greet us like old friends.

We ended up playing three Day on the Green shows for Bill, but I still can picture that first as if it were yesterday. I remember how we were driven into the bowels of the stadium, which was like a giant concrete bowl, and being able to hear the noise of the crowd from backstage. There were three other acts on the bill that day: Peter Frampton, Fleetwood Mac, who'd just become stars in America, and an American singer-songwriter, Gary Wright. Each of us had our own trailer backstage. We didn't hang out with the other acts, kept to ourselves, but I did run into Stevie Nicks in the artists' toilets behind the stage.

Stevie was at her most beautiful at that time, before she fell prey to the dreaded white powder. Glamorous wouldn't come close to describing how good she looked. I was just having a wander, getting my head together for the show, and she said hello to me. Stevie and Lindsey Buckingham were obviously still an item at the time, but I tell you what, the mere fact that she even gave the time of day to me was tantamount to a marriage proposal. I was left floating on air. I didn't press things with her any further, though; wouldn't have wanted to make a fool of myself. Within a year Fleetwood Mac would have released their *Rumours* album and become the biggest band in the world. We did two or three more huge shows with them out in California at that time. After the last one of those, I remember that we had to drive through the night to get up to Canada to do a gig of our own the next day. En route, we rendezvoused with a drug dealer at a truck stop and took delivery of a suitcase filled with prime-quality cocaine. I don't believe it even lasted the rest of that journey.

At the Coliseum, it was seven in the evening when we walked on stage and the sun was still out. I didn't have any fear or nerves. It seemed to me as if everybody in the stadium had been waiting just for us. We got an ovation even before we had played a note, but then we always did in San Francisco. This, though, was a truly great line-up of the band; perhaps the best. We had a terrific singer in Phil Mogg, a rock-solid drummer, Andy Parker, and a blond-haired, blue-eyed German genius of a guitarist, Michael Schenker. And then there was me on Thunderbird bass, my face framed by two curtains of black hair, running about from one side of the vast stage to the other, a blur of manic energy. The experience of playing to that many people wasn't really any different to doing an arena show, and by then we'd done plenty of those to crowds who went wild for us every night. I'd begun to get used to such a reception in America and only ever really concentrated on the faces down at the front. If those guys looked as if they were having a good time, then I knew the rest of the crowd would be all right too. Just as we would do at the Winterland Ballroom and countless more shows in America and around the world over the next two or three years, we bowled over the Coliseum crowd and left them wanting more. It felt as if we were indestructible, unstoppable and on top of the world.

Initially, I was acutely aware of how far I'd come in just five or six years, from practising in my bedroom at my parents' flat in Enfield to this – rock stardom. Quite honestly, when we first got off the plane to the States in 1975 and opened up shows for Steppenwolf, I thought then that I'd made it. But once I'd got past that point, I didn't think we were in competition any more with the other up-and-coming British bands. They could sell a few hundred tickets in London, whereas we measured ourselves against the big boys, the superstars. We were very, very good, too, there's no doubt about it, and we knew it.

That period as a whole was amazing for me, like riding the crest of a wave. I knew we were on the cusp of achieving something very special and lasting, but I don't think I was aware of just how big a band we could have been. It was great simply to be out on tour and to play to thousands of people a night, and to have this sense that America, the home of rock and roll, was breaking for us. There was an adrenalin rush from the shows, of course there was, but also from the fun that went right along with them.

I got to act out all of my schoolboy fantasies and felt as if I was on top of the world. And it didn't seem even conceivable to me that this rollercoaster ride I was on would ever come to a stop, or that I could possibly allow any of this magical, wondrous stuff to be snatched away from me.

PART ONE:
Lift-Off

CHAPTER 1

*Of growing up in suburbia, the first fumbling encounters
with girls, and the curse of model railways as
articulated by one Ozzy Osbourne.*

―――――

The first thing I can ever remember is our flat on Enfield Road. This was the 1950s and most of the buildings in the Enfield area had been bombed during the war. Growing up I shared a bedroom with my younger brother, Neill. Neill is five years younger than me and can remember all the things I can't, which is a lot. The two of us had football posters up on the walls and as we got older combined our vinyl record collections. Both of us grew up with music.

Mum and Dad were Ruth and Fred. They had both served in the war. Dad was in the Air Force and stationed in Egypt and Mum was in the Land Army. Dad served at El Alamein. I admired both of them for what they went through. Dad once told me about being on a troop ship that sailed from Egypt to South Africa. He made it sound as if it was the most wonderful

experience and yet it occurred to me later that at any moment
he could have been sunk by a German U-boat. He loved boats
all of his life. They bought a house in Dover after Dad retired
and he would spend hours just watching boats sail in and out
of the harbour.

Mum was a housewife and Dad worked as a sales manager. I
came along four years after they got married. They were good,
kind parents and their hearts were in the right place. But they
had that sense of military discipline instilled in them from the
age of eighteen and didn't suffer fools. They never wanted me
to be a fool that was for sure. Overall, it was a middle-class
upbringing and I didn't want for anything, but it was strict,
too. Neill and I were brought up to be young adults and always
to say please and thank you. As children, we were expected
to be smart in our appearance. Each summer, like a religion,
Mum and Dad would troop us into town to buy our school
uniforms. It might as well have been a military uniform,
because they dealt with me as if I were a lowly private in
their army. I went to Merryhills Primary School. It was a nice
school with well-behaved kids and in a good area. As such, I
didn't get into any particular scrapes as a youngster. But if I had
I certainly wouldn't have dared to tell Mum or Dad. Later on
in life, Dad was appalled at how much money I would spend
on drink and drugs. We used to row a lot. The horses were
his hobby, so in reply I'd ask him how much he'd lost lately
on having a bet. He and Mum both lived to a ripe old age. I
think they were both baffled at how it was that I managed to
survive. They thought I was ready for the next life by the time
I was in my thirties.

Neill Way, Pete's younger brother: Mum and Dad were very supportive and good to us. Dad worked for a plastics company up in Waltham Cross and once I went to primary school, Mum got a job at the school as a dinner lady. It really was quite difficult growing up with Pete. He was the one who gave Mum and Dad the most trouble, that's the truth. The two of us used to get on reasonably well, but because of the five-year age gap I was the one who always got knocked around. Growing up, we didn't actually do that much together. We lived just a quarter of a mile from the local park, so in the school holidays I'd go down there for a kick-about with my mates while Pete would be off doing whatever it was he got up to with his friends, but probably no good. The one thing that he was passionate about at that point was model railways.

True enough, from five years old I was obsessed with model railways. Mum used to take me trainspotting to New Barnet station, I even had a little book to write numbers in, and Dad got me a train set for my birthday – a Hornby Princess Elizabeth set. That was one of the great moments in my life. It was cheap, cheerful, but God, it didn't half give me some hours of fun. I used to get up at the crack of dawn to start the first train of the day running around the track and I'd save up all of my pocket money just to buy new engines. It had to be steam engines, too. At my age, when diesel trains came along they seemed a bit dull by comparison. I still collect model trains even now. I've even been on eBay and outbid other people to get hold of an A4 LNER Pacific.

Sadly, you can't be a trainspotter and a rock-and-roll degenerate at the same time. Eventually, my pocket money started to go on clothes and then on nights out to London.

But it's a passion and I've never lost my love for the railways. Matter of fact, I know that Rod Stewart, Eric Clapton and Roger Daltrey also build their own railways, and Neil Young even bought his own model railway company, Lionel Trains. I once brought the subject up with Ozzy Osbourne. We were on a tour bus at the time and he actually got quite upset about it. He told me that his dad had collected model trains and had died. Then he started to cry. He was literally sobbing and blurted out to me, 'Pete, don't collect trains, don't do it, they're bad luck.' I couldn't console him. We probably ended up having another drink.

I passed the eleven-plus and went to George Spicer Grammar School. The school was in quite a grand old building and highly respected in the area. I didn't know Phil Mogg then, but he went to the rough school down the road, Bush Hill Park Secondary. The two schools used to be rivals and there would be fights between both sets of pupils over in the park that separated the respective buildings, so much so that it was eventually made out of bounds. Grammar school was great fun up until the third year, when they started to throw exams at us. By then I think my friends and I had managed to drag George Spicer's reputation down. We would do silly, harmless stuff like bring plastic bows into class and fire the arrows up into the ceiling. Or hide out in the bicycle sheds and make off with other kids' or even the teachers' bikes.

I sort of gravitated to the kids who were there to be caned. I also got the cane on several occasions, but not for doing anything serious. If I had done, my parents would have killed me. There was one time when my mates and I pushed a parked car over on our walk home from school. My more regular pranks were to hide the teachers' briefcases outside the windows of their classrooms, or else let the tyres down on their cars.

Otherwise, I spent my first three years at George Spicer handing my homework in late and growing my hair. The headmaster, Mr Gowers, would constantly inspect our hair length. If it grew over your ears, he would give you half a crown to go into town and have it cut. On one occasion, a couple of mates and I went off to the barber and asked for crew cuts. When I came back into school Mr Gowers told me I was the stupidest person he had ever met, which says a lot.

Mum and Dad went on being sticklers for uniform and forced me to wear these awful pleated grey trousers to school. My mates obviously took the piss out of me, but I learned to sew and made a spare pair of trousers into drainpipes. I hid them under a hedge two minutes' walk from home and each morning would get changed into them on the way to school. I was kind of a Mod in a way, what with my tight-fitting trousers and growing my hair out. We might also have launched the punk rock fashion trend at George Spicer. This daft craze started with pulling the pockets off other kids' blazers. That soon progressed to pulling peoples' sleeves off and ripping off their lapels. My mum would be bewildered when I came home with the perfectly good blazer that she and Dad had just bought for me, torn to shreds. The punk-rock thing about it was that we would all use safety pins to fix our pockets and lapels back on.

George Spicer was a mixed-sex school, too. That was my first experience of really getting to *know* girls. After that, I never again felt awkward being around the fairer sex. The girls' playground was separate to the boys', but we would meet at the bike sheds. My mates and I used to play this game to see if we could get one of the girls to take her blouse off, and with occasional success. You grew up fast at thirteen. However, I didn't have a serious girlfriend all through school. I used to flirt with some of the girls and had crushes, but I was a bit shy in that respect. I didn't really see myself as being much of a catch.

To me, it was also almost as if girls would drag, or else slow you down. Back then it was very much about going out with your mates and you would have to interrupt that routine in order to take a girl to the pictures. The good thing was that I had a paper round, a milk round and a Saturday job at Woolworths, so for such occasions I was able to buy a new shirt or record and make it look as if I were the richest kid in Enfield. See, the girls at school were always happy to be taken out by older guys who had jobs, so you had to try and compete. I was good at putting up a front, still am, but behind the act there was in reality an extremely worried young man.

———

I would always kick a ball around in the playground and my grandfather had been general secretary of Enfield Football Club, so my aunt used to take me along to see them play on a Saturday afternoon. I loved going to the football and that was the start of another of my life-long passions. In general, Mum and Dad encouraged me to do sport. I was also quite a good middle-distance runner and joined a local club, Ponders End Athletics Club. Two mornings a week before school, I'd cycle down to the club to go training.

I won medals at cross-country, too. That was quite exciting and also character building. For a while I was fully committed to my running and it kept me on the straight and narrow, which pleased Mum and Dad no end. Of course, as soon as I discovered music, that was a whole different outlook on life and running kind of fizzled out for me. That was the turning point at which I veered off from being the nice boy who cut the grass and would help the milkman and started to realize there was a whole other world out there.

Neill Way: I've still got boxes filled with stuff from Mum and Dad's flat, which I had to clear out when Mum passed away. They had kept all of Pete's medals from various athletics events and where he'd come in second or third. He used to do the mile and was a reasonably good runner. He would also go down to places like White City and help to marshal at the major athletics events. He had a book that he filled up with the autographs of all of the famous runners of the time. Later on, the fact he was a keen athlete definitely came across in how he performed on stage.

The first time I became even aware of music I was watching the telly with my parents and Elvis Presley came on singing 'Jailhouse Rock'. That dum-dum, duh-duh beat is about as close to Led Zeppelin and hard rock as it's possible to get. It just instantly grabbed hold of me. I started to listen to early Elvis and then when I was a teenager the Beatles arrived on the scene. A friend of mine, Alan Payne, would get all of the Beatles' early singles. Ironically enough, Alan went on to become one of the chief customs officials in the country. I often wonder how Alan would have reacted if he had known what I ended up bringing into the country with me. Then, of course, the Rolling Stones came along and that was it for me. I liked the Fab Four well enough, but if I was going to be anybody it was a Rolling Stone. They were the first band that *got* me, and then it was the Who, the Kinks, the Pretty Things and another group from the London scene called the Creation.

At thirteen, I started to get the steam train from Enfield into London with a couple of friends to go to the Marquee Club on a Saturday night. We were really just naïve schoolkids hanging around the West End, but it was so exciting. The bands we went to see could have played anything and I would have loved it. The Marquee itself wasn't exactly overwhelming as a venue, in fact it was quite grotty, but everybody we met was friendly to us and the atmosphere of the place was just fantastic. I don't think there was anybody I saw at the Marquee that I didn't think was at least good. At the end of the night, we would have to hotfoot it to Liverpool Street station to make the last train back to Enfield, and it was quite a walk from there to our flat. Some nights we would miss the train and all hell would break loose when I did at last pitch up at home the next morning.

I saw so many bands and artists at the Marquee who were just then starting out and it was that which gave me my inspiration. I saw Jimi Hendrix over and again and also the Small Faces. I would even go along to catch the Bonzo Dog Doo Dah Band just to be able to see something different and funnier, but I developed a taste for hard rock. I saw the New Yardbirds make their debut at the Marquee, and of course they turned into Led Zeppelin, and found myself overwhelmed by their sheer power. Above all else, it was seeing them that night

18

that really made me focus on wanting to achieve something with music.

Back in Enfield I began to hang around the town centre with a group of lads. I wouldn't say it was a gang as such, but the ringleaders were very much the sort of blokes who went around and looked to start fights. They were good with their fists as well, whereas I was more accomplished at being stood behind someone else whenever any trouble kicked off. In Enfield back then, you were either a part of the in-crowd or an outsider, and if you were out your life could be made a misery. There was a group of skinheads and then a bunch of other lads who were more like rockers or Mods. If one lot or the other didn't know your face you would get mercilessly bullied. I flitted between being a Mod and really wanting to dress like Mick Jagger, but I kept out of harm's way. The lads I knew always appeared to be very self-confident and I suppose that rubbed off on me too. I was determined at the same time not to be one of the thugs. Four or five years later, I would drive through the town centre and see those same lads stood outside the same pubs, still on the lookout for who they were going to kick off with next. I was also fortunate in the fact that both of my cousins were well known for their ability to take care of themselves. They were seen as the leaders of the gang and basically looked after me. In actual fact, all that testosterone stuff was quite exciting but by then all that I really thought about was music. Whenever I wasn't down at the Marquee, I would go to this poky little place in Enfield called the Blues Room to see all the local bands and drink cider.

Of course, there were also drugs about. Eight or nine of us would go round to the house of this slightly older guy, Jerry.

Jerry's parents always seemed to be away for some reason. It was a real hippy environment, not that we were hippies. Everybody would bring along different albums to Jerry's, which is how I started to listen to all those early Californian bands such as the Doors, Jefferson Airplane and Love. We would stay up all night doing acid and Dexedrine. Acid didn't have any effect on me other than to make me daft. There would be lots of hash doing the rounds, too, but I was never that into smoking pot. I hated the smell of it for one thing.

But that was the thing about drugs: from an early age everyone I knew and hung around with took them so I didn't ever see them as being dangerous or taboo. In fact it was quite the opposite – doing drugs was made to me to seem normal, almost run-of-the-mill – and the simple fact was that I grew very quickly to enjoy them. Even back in those formative years I saw myself as being something of a connoisseur. So in my mind the more drugs I got to experience, the better.

Right from that age I was also around people who were routinely doing smack, and I wanted to try it too. I took the view that it would be part of my ongoing education. I was thirteen when I got my first shot of heroin. An older guy hit me up, and straight away I preferred it to anything else that I'd had to that point. It made me feel sick for sure, but that was beside the point. It was as if I had tasted Utopia, though it would eventually turn around and bite me back.

When I was at Jerry's I wouldn't get home till six or seven the next morning, and then I'd have to face a court martial from my parents. 'Where have you been? What have you been up to and who with?' It was a nuisance to me at the time, but I realize now that Mum and Dad had just wanted to raise me properly. Most of the time I even let them think that they were succeeding. The sad truth is, though, that five or six of the guys who hung around at Jerry's were dead before they were eighteen, including the lad who gave me that first shot of heroin. My mum would clip out a front-page story in the *Enfield Gazette* about one or other of them having died from an overdose. But by that point I was in a band and off on tour, so I wasn't touched by their stories or what it might mean for me – not at all.

Round about the time I was sixteen, a mate of mine got a guitar. That had an immediate effect on me. Soon enough, I stopped going down to the athletics club twice a week to do an eight-mile training run. From that point on, there was nothing that was more inspirational to me than having my own guitar and the prospect of being able to put a band together and write songs. As luck would have it, one Saturday afternoon right around then and through a mutual friend, I was introduced to Phil Mogg. Phil was a year older than me, and very precious about the clothes he bought and how he looked. He seemed to me loud, brash and confident, and even then was never shy of having a drink or two. To begin with, in fact, I thought he was arrogant, a bit too sure of himself. Like me, though, Phil's total, all-consuming hobby was music. And he had one important contact, a guy who would go and score acid for us. That was the true beginning of our friendship.

However, for all that I had started to run wild, I did eventually fall into line at school and buckled down to academic work. I ended up passing most of my exams pretty well, in the main to defy the teachers who hadn't given me a hope in hell of getting a good job. I particularly liked History and was pretty good at French too. We used to go to France for family holidays in the summer and had relatives in Belgium, so it was an advantage to be able to speak the language. And best of all, when I got a little older it was never an issue for me to score drugs in France.

CHAPTER 2

*In which a drunken escapade is had, a pleasing side effect
of sleeping pills is discovered and the inadvertent
arson of a steel factory is brought about.*

———

I was never too popular with my mates in Enfield, because more
often than not I would return their records to them scratched.
What would happen was that I'd buy one album and a mate
another and then the pair of us would swap. The first record
I bought with my own money was one of those early Kinks
singles: 'You Really Got Me' or 'All Day and All of the Night'.
Then I got hold of the first albums by the Rolling Stones and
the Who. Mum and Dad got me a record player for my sixteenth
birthday, nothing special, but to me there was something truly
exciting about being able to close my bedroom door and make
a racket. From that moment on, a continuous battle went on in
our flat between Dad and me over volume. Each confrontation,
though, would be brought to an end by the stomp of Dad's feet
down the corridor to my room.

Everybody I hung around with was into music, whether they wanted to look like somebody in a band, or actually aspired to play. At that age, it wasn't so much that I had ambitions to be a bass player. I just wanted to able to play something, anything. And four strings were quicker for me to pick up, especially as I had friends who were better than me at guitar. Ever since then, I've never taken the guitar much further than being able to manage the simplest chords. I did try to master more back then, but never took to it.

Neill Way: I can remember when Pete first started to learn guitar with his Bert Weedon Play in a Day *book. He would try to get me to sing some of the songs for him to play along to, old folk stuff like 'On Top of Old Smokey'. If you've ever heard Pete sing, all that needs to be said is that I had an even worse voice.*

Even with the bass, I'm not one for playing as fast as possible. What I learned was how to keep my bass lines solid so that the lead guitarist would have something to play around. I had all the usual heroes and influences: John Paul Jones from Led Zeppelin, Bill Wyman of the Stones, and later on, Black Sabbath's Geezer Butler. The one thing I never wanted to emulate, though, was Bill's stage performance. I mean to say, he looked like he was nailed to the floor. I was never going to be satisfied with a role in the background.

I probably borrowed my first bass from a friend, or else nicked it. Either way, I didn't actually buy it and it was utter rubbish, which is why I never bothered to learn how to tune it. But I was diligent about practising. Well, sort of diligent. I spent pretty much every evening in my bedroom messing around on my new toy. I would attempt to plonk along to my records, but in reality all that I hoped to do was to get a grip of the easier bits. It wasn't until I started playing with a guitarist that I gradually worked out the harder parts and even then I would play them in my own particular way.

I met Mick Bolton one Saturday night with the acid crowd. He was a good guitarist and we became fast friends, even though all we ever talked about was music. You could say that Mick and I grew up together as musicians. He lived near to me up on Winchmore Hill and most nights from then on I would go round to his house with my bass and we'd play along together. Being naïve, I didn't realize you had to tune the bass to the rhythm guitar. God knows what the din we used to make was like for his parents, but even to us it sounded as if we were playing three different songs at once. Eventually, the two of us began to write songs. They were pretty rudimentary, but there's nothing like coming up with your own material to improve your abilities. That's how you learn the tricks of the trade. The next step was to play with other people. It was nothing serious at that point. We'd ask around our mates to see if anyone else wanted to have a bash and then go around to, say, a drummer's house because his folks wouldn't mind us practising there. Mick and I were constantly on the lookout for kids who were more gifted than us, but there were none as determined. That being said, the two of us didn't do anything outside of our bedrooms or a garage. The Boyfriends was our first proper group and even that came together in Mick's mum and dad's front room. Mick and I also sang and we got in a guy called Tic Torino to drum for us. Tic was Italian and his parents ran a very nice restaurant up in the West End. He could just about keep up a basic four-four beat, but in the main Tic got the gig because his folks would let us rehearse for hours at a time at their house.

The best way I can sum up the average drummer's status in a band is through a funny story I once heard about Aynsley Dunbar, who much later on I would play with in UFO. Now, Aynsley was a great drummer and had played with the likes of Frank Zappa, Lou Reed and David Bowie. He was also a member of the American band Journey just before they broke into the big time. Journey had an outstanding singer as well, Steve Perry, and the trouble was that Aynsley hated him. Apparently, Aynsley ended up going to the band's management and giving them an ultimatum: it was either him or Perry. What do you think they were going to do? Ditch the guy with a seven-octave range or the bloke who goes bump-boom-boom? Of course, Aynsley got the boot.

Tic was just as invaluable to our band, though the Boyfriends were basically a wannabe pop group. I used to wear my best rock-and-roll clothes, but to begin with at least we sounded more like the Hollies. We were, though, very enthusiastic. We would rehearse two to three times a week, at Tic's house or in the bedroom Neill and I shared until a neighbour complained to Dad about the noise.

Neill Way: I can still picture the Boyfriends practising in our bedroom on Sunday afternoons. The lady next door came to see Dad and told him that she was being rocked in her bath, which put an end to their sessions. But both Mum and Dad took a particular interest in Pete's music. Dad arranged for the band to rehearse every Saturday afternoon in an empty office at the place where he worked. Dad would drive them down to Waltham Cross, and I'd have to sit outside in the car with him and Mum until they had finished. Dad always said, though, that he wanted Pete to get a proper job.

All through his life my dad got the greatest pleasure out of being asked what his Peter's band was up to. Years later he would come and see me play with UFO at the Hammersmith Odeon, but that made him a terrible wreck. He would be sat with Mum upstairs in the dress circle and fret about what might go wrong. I tried to tell him that it was harder for me to play for twenty people in a pub. Mostly, I think Mum and Dad were kind of intrigued by what I was up to and also pleased that I'd got a hobby. To their way of thinking, music kept me away from the riff-raff. That wasn't strictly true, since Phil was still part of the picture. Every so often the Boyfriends would do a college or youth club gig to twenty or thirty people and Phil would come down to see us. In fact, he was always on the scene and if we rehearsed, say, a Cream song, Phil would invariably be stood behind us and start to sing along. Mick and I didn't necessarily have distinctive voices, so it became obvious that we needed a proper singer and also that Phil did actually sound like Jack Bruce. Eventually, we asked Phil to join us and that moved along the whole concept of the band. The sound toughened up and we changed our name to Hocus Pocus, a second consecutive terrible name. I had just then discovered an American band called Blue Cheer and their version of Eddie Cochran's 'Summertime Blues' was a big influence on our new, harder approach. That song was so primal, and heavy, it sounded to me like the work of cavemen.

Phil would always volunteer to drive the van to our gigs, but had an ulterior motive. He would suggest the rest of us unload and set up the gear, while he went off to get a parking place. Typically, he would then park up the van as far as was possible from the venue. Of course, by the time he finally made it back we would have done all the heavy lifting and there would be nothing left for him to do. Phil never seemed to go short either. Even when the rest of us were flat broke and the band's petrol and snacks fund had been exhausted, he would somehow still be flush.

I think because he was that bit older Phil sort of naturally gravitated to taking charge of the group. Without him, though, we wouldn't have had anyone to steer us in a particular direction. Phil was very precise in expressing what he thought, very self-assured, and where he led the rest of us undoubtedly followed. He could certainly have his moods and sulk, but Phil is probably the only person I've ever taken any notice of or listened to in the slightest. He has also led me up all kinds of dark alleys, but the two of us grew to be very tight. From the very beginning, Phil would always try to look and act the part. He was like a rock star in training. At rehearsals, each of us would want to do our best to please him. He would sit there and listen intently to an idea, like a presiding judge, and you would only know if he liked it or not if he could be bothered to get up and sing. The two of us could talk together all night and we each had an endless supply of jokes, but at the same time, if Phil wasn't happy about something I'd done he would not hesitate to jump down my throat.

———

After leaving school I got a job as a junior clerk at a maritime insurance company in the City of London. It was pretty boring. Anybody can fill out a form and since I had passed all these exams at school, it felt to me like a waste of my time. Worse still, I had to wear a suit and tie. I had two work suits. One was dark and the other pinstriped. I also bought a flash lilac number that Mick Jagger might have worn. I certainly wouldn't have been allowed to sport that to work, so it was reserved exclusively for the weekends. It was otherwise one of my great pleasures in life to be able to tear my work suit off and pull on a pair of jeans when I got home.

One of my daily duties was to walk over to Customs House with the document that listed all of the boats and cargo that were being insured that day and that was how I first met Yvonne. She worked at Customs House as a secretary and would have to stamp this document. For me it was instant attraction, but then she was very pretty. She still is today from the photographs of her that I've seen, which is remarkable in a way. On account of me, I'm stunned that she hasn't at least got a head full of grey hair. Yvonne and I got to talking, as you do when you see someone every day, but 'Can you stamp this for me?' was hardly the best chat-up line. Finally, though, I worked up the courage to ask her out to lunch and it carried on from there. And by the time of our second date to the cinema, I had got my patter worked out, too.

Really and truly, Yvonne was my first proper girlfriend. Up to that point, my whole focus had been on music and then on the band. I'd picked up the odd girl here and there at a pub or club, but nothing serious and there hadn't been a great deal of sex involved. It wasn't as if I was naïve in that respect, I had just been too preoccupied with making time to practise or else hanging out with my band mates. Along the way, I met so many guys who were set upon a career in music, but got married instead. Even at that early stage, I would never have given up on my dream for a girl.

To begin with at least, Yvonne and I got on great. She liked music, so I took her with me to see Zeppelin at the Albert Hall and also to the Marquee and my other regular haunts. I suppose you could say she was the love of my life, or at least my first love. She must have been, because we ended up getting married. That was how it was at the time. Once the two of you had been going out for six months or so, both sets of parents and her friends would start to ask when you planned to get engaged. Somehow or other, though, Yvonne never did share my conviction that I would also go on to be famous.

After just a few months, I left my post at the insurance company and got another job as a civil servant with the Ministry of Defence. I was based on Horse Guards Parade and was told that one of the perks of working there was being able to watch the Trooping the Colour ceremony from the office window. It might sound quite a grand position, but in reality it was just another lowly clerical role. As opposed to doing anything of great national import, I filed paperwork all day. That aside, all that I did in the office was talk about my favourite bands with the other junior members of staff. I spent a further year there until I found out from a friend who worked as a petrol pump attendant that he was able to make as much as me on tips alone. The only advantage to being a civil servant that I was able to see was that I could take extremely long lunch breaks. That allowed me enough time to hand-deliver the Boyfriends' dreadful demo cassettes to record companies in the West End, to which 'We'll let you know' was the typical response. In fact, I was gone so long and often from the MOD that my boss insisted I see a social worker to establish whether or not I had personal issues. Ten years too soon, he thought I was an alcoholic or else a drug addict.

My meagre wage at least meant I was able to leave home at seventeen. Phil, Mick, Tic and I got a house together just down the road from Mum and Dad's in Bounds Green. All four of us contributed to the rent, but Phil took care of the brunt of it because his job paid the best. By that time, he was employed as a trainee carpet layer. He even had his own van, which was useful to the band, though there were always rolls of carpet stuffed in the back. Funnily enough, years later and whenever we checked into a five-star hotel, Phil would critique the carpets. 'The bloke who laid that has done a bloody shoddy job,' he would say, sagely. 'Will you look at the state of the edges and joins?' There was nothing outstanding about our new home. It was an average, semi-detached house of the kind you find in countless suburban north London streets. Certainly, every other house on our road looked the same, although it did at least face out on to a little green. Mick and Tic had their own rooms, while Phil and I shared, which would soon enough become common practice for the pair of us. Ours was the biggest room and with a double bed, which we also had to share. Every now and again, Phil and I would both bring girls back and all of us would end up between the sheets. Even then, I found it all but impossible to be faithful to just one girl.

The owner of the house was a Greek gentleman, Mr Nicola. He was quite tolerant, but now and again would pop round to chase up the rent or else demonstrate to us how to work a lawnmower. Tending the lawn wasn't high on our list of priorities and the back garden was usually so overgrown you could get lost in the long grass. We did, though, establish a cleaning rota, but Phil was the only one of us who ever bothered to stick to it. Phil was freakish about cleanliness and kept the inside of the house spotless. If one or other of Mick, Tic and I left dirty plates piled up in the kitchen sink, Phil would do his nut, but then wash them up and scrub the floor to boot. On Sunday lunchtimes, I'd go round to Mum and Dad's to get a decent meal. Dad would drop me back off afterwards and, thank God, never asked to come into the house, because often as not it was also inhabited by all kinds of other degenerates. I would never know who else was going to be there or what they might be up to. In particular, I remember one Glaswegian guy who Phil knew. His name was John and Phil had told us that if a John ever knocked on the door, to not under any circumstance allow him over the threshold. Naturally, he did turn up late one night and, of course, I inadvertently let him into the house.

After that, John and another ne'er-do-well mate of his, known to us only as Alan, basically moved in to our house. Not only that, but the two of them also started to run a makeshift business from the premises, screening porn movies in our front room and charging a bunch of blokes from the pub to come in and watch them. Many were the times I got home from work to find a leering gang of men sat around our telly with a crate of beer. John even had the audacity to ask the four of us to make out that we were paying customers if we happened to be home during one of his film soirées. Neither John nor Alan ever paid us any rent, even with their illicit business going strong. Phil would go mental about that, but blamed me for being idiot enough to open up the door to them in the first place. They were a couple of right thieves, too, and in the end nicked all of our band gear. I'll never forget that incident, because it was on the same day that the Stones played in Hyde Park: 5 July 1969. I came home to find all of our instruments gone and so too were John and his pal.

A motley collection of friends and assorted other people would also be regulars round the house. To be sociable, we kept a big glass jar full of pills on a table in the front room. The big thing at the time was Mandrax. It was one of the strongest sleeping tablets you could get hold of in Britain, before that is it got banned from sale. In America, the tablets were called Quaaludes, though Mandrax were even stronger. I took them all the time back then, and particularly with Dexedrine, since they worked very well together. With Mandy's, if you could get past the falling asleep bit and avoid passing out, they made you feel nicely wobbly and also uninhibited. It was on account of this second effect that we used to call them Randy Mandy's and were especially generous whenever we doled them out to our female guests.

Increasingly, there didn't seem to me to be any downside to doing drugs. As I judged it, they made me feel good and also attractive to the opposite sex, so what was not to like? Besides the odd pint of cider, I didn't drink a whole lot in those days but I developed a very strong constitution for sleeping pills and speed. In actual fact, I wish that I'd known then what I do now, which is that if you do speed exclusively then it's better to have a drink at the same time because that will help to mellow

33

you out. I was always a get-up-and-go type of person and Dexedrine only intensified that, to the point where I couldn't sit still even for a second.

It perhaps goes without saying, but we had a wild time in Bounds Green. We would throw acid parties, having gone to the Roundhouse in Camden and brought home a crowd of people who had nothing better to do. There would be thirty or so lads, none of whom we knew, crashed out downstairs, or else a group of Dutch girls scattered about our bedrooms. I wasn't so much of a one for psychedelics, but we were careful and took precautions. The only pictures we hung in the house were subdued in colour, landscapes mostly, not the sort of things likely to turn into terrifying monsters when you were tripping. Plus, we had the green outside so no one was very likely to wander off in front of a car. The police would quite often park up on the road outside, but only because of the noise. Loud music would blare out from the house pretty much all day and we'd hold band practice at our house. Whenever a police car did turn up on the scene, the four us would frantically try to hide our stash of pills. Unfortunately, Tic in the end was driven to a nervous breakdown by his speed intake. I think it was Black Bombers that did for him. They were these little black tablets, quite potent as the name suggests, and he just took far too many of them. Basically, he went totally off the rails and we couldn't communicate with him. He went back home to his parents' to be looked after. Poor Tic eventually recovered, but we lost touch with him. I wasn't unduly alarmed by Tic's unravelling, but then, I firmly believed that I was more tolerant of drugs and not so reckless.

Phil, Mick and I met Andy Parker through an old school

friend of mine at George Spicer. I bumped into this lad one night in a pub and he happened to be with Andy. At the time, Andy was still living with his parents in Cheshunt in Hertfordshire and attended the local college. In fact, he got us a gig there which paid a fiver, enough to cover the petrol and a bag of fish and chips between us. After that, Andy started to come along to see us play at pubs and youth clubs in our local area. Andy's father was a craftsman and the great thing was he had passed on his knowledge of electrics to his son. To our general astonishment, Andy was able to rewire all of our gear so that it sounded markedly better. If anything so much as buzzed, Andy would shout up in his nasally, Hertfordshire accent, 'Leave that to me', and have it fixed in minutes. If Phil's van broke down in the middle of nowhere, Andy would leap out and get under the bonnet while the rest of us kept warm.

Soon enough, Phil made Andy a deal that if he would agree to roadie for us we would pay him the princely sum of nothing. Andy accepted without hesitation, which doubtless sealed his future fate in the band. One night soon afterwards we had Andy set up and check the drum kit, and off he went, hitting it really hard and with no little skill. A guy who could solder cables *and* play the drums? It was like a dream come true. Andy was a great character, too. He was always very serious about everything, which of course Phil and I thought was hilarious. So often did he ask the two of us, completely bemused, 'What's so fucking funny?' that it became his catchphrase.

With Andy on board, the band definitely stepped up another level. Black Sabbath had also broken through by then and that was the final piece of the puzzle to how we wanted to sound. Hocus Pocus obviously didn't do justice to such hard-rocking music, so we changed our name once again, on this occasion to UFO. It was Phil who came up with it, and I believe he took it from the psychedelic club in the West End where Pink Floyd had started out. We had written our own material from the beginning, but now also began to focus on being able to put on a proper performance. I don't suppose we did anything more than emulate our musical heroes, but in public at least we started to look very sure of ourselves. Competent enough at any rate to get ourselves picked up by two managers, Terry Collins and Johnny Spence. Johnny had been bassist with Johnny Kidd and the Pirates, one of the better known of the many beat groups to have come out of London in the Swinging Sixties. He taught me an awful lot about stage presence and how each person has a responsibility for their section of the stage.

For all the new-found optimism that surged through the band's ranks, we needed to earn more money to buy better gear and so Mick and I got work as labourers at a stainless steel factory. It paid very well for a seventeen-year-old, enough for us to pick up four Marshall Stacks, Mick a Fender Telecaster and me a Fender Precision bass. Dad was good enough to sign the HP form for the Marshalls. Had he not, UFO might not have continued to exist. At work, the only labouring that Mick and I did was to run off to the tool shed. The two of us, together with a Pakistani lad of our age, would spend each day hidden away in there, smoking dope. None of the actual craftsmen could be bothered to try and find us, so they would end up doing our job as well, which was to unload the delivery lorries. Fortunately for us, they were a good-natured bunch and Mick and I would tell them all about how the band was doing to keep them onside. That was a good early lesson for me in just how interesting a musician can make himself appear to other people. Subsequently, I put it to very good use. Our band aside, though, our fellow workers must have thought the two of us a waste of space.

It was on that job that I got drunk for the first time. It was the middle of summer, and in our lunch hour Mick and I went out and bought a bottle of scrumpy cider. Sat out in the sun, we polished it off in no time. Next thing, I threw up all over the place. For the rest of the day, I was even more hopeless than usual and didn't like the feeling of being drunk at all. In the end, the floor manager actually sent me home, thinking I'd got sunstroke. It would take a gallon of scrumpy to have anything like the same effect on me these days. But after that, whenever I passed out on the job from smoking dope or drinking too much booze, I would claim to have sunstroke, even if it was pissing down with rain.

On another ill-starred occasion, I almost set fire to the factory. There was a drainage system that ran around the entire building and on this particular day it had filled up with rainwater. For a reason lost to me now, I decided it would be fun to stage a re-enactment of the Battle of Trafalgar and to use boats made out of folded-up pages of newspaper. I spent a lot of time making my armada, and then floated it off around the drains. What I hadn't realized, though, was that a certain amount of oil and chemicals were also being drained off. Since there was a battle meant to be going on, I struck a match and set fire to one of my makeshift boats. Blow me, one whole wall of the building went up in flames and fire shot up to the very roof. The people at work nearby must have wondered why Mick and I all of a sudden started to run around like madmen, with fire buckets filled with sand, but by then they thought better of asking us what we were up to. The things you do when you have nothing to do.

Not long after that, our time in Bounds Green also came to a premature end. A lot of families also lived on our street. We'd never actually spoken to any of our neighbours, because I think they steered well clear of us: the mad people up the road. However, a majority of our fellow residents eventually got fed up with the noise and general comings and goings at our house. It wasn't as if we had tried to annoy them, but just for one thing we would practise at hours that perhaps weren't convenient for regular people. And although we would start off with our amps on 'one', this would inevitably creep up and we would end in the middle of the night at full blast. After months of being subjected to this hideous din, our neighbours collectively got up a petition to have us evicted. Phil took on the role of chief executive in our delicate negotiations with Mr Nicola, but was unable to stop us from being thrown out of the house. I went back to my parents' flat, which was no bad thing for me. It was easy enough for me to get the bus from there down to the steel factory and the band was doing gigs on a more regular basis, so had improved no end.

We had, in fact, got to be pretty good. Good enough at least for us to make a major investment. We bought our own Transit van and Andy fitted it out with old airline seats. Sat in that van, I really did think that I was on my way.

CHAPTER 3

The road to discovery throws up a young German wizard,
a predatory experience in a cellar and an
ill-timed dose of gonorrhoea.

———

Terry Collins and Johnny Spence eventually talked a guy named Milton Samuels into giving us a record deal with his independent label, Beacon Records. Andy was still so young that his parents had to countersign the contract for him and none of us was well versed in the practicalities of such things. We didn't know it then, but the deal wasn't worth a bean to us. In our minds, the only thing that mattered was that we would get all of our studio time paid for and so be able to record our first album.

We were taken in by Milton, since he was a larger-than-life character. A black fella who liked his funk music, Milton had previously signed an American soul band, the Show Stoppers, and had a hit with them back in 1967 with a song called 'Ain't Nothing but a House Party'. I think Milton had convinced himself that Beacon ought to have a rock band too, but he wouldn't have known the difference between a good and bad one. He did, though, have all the talk. He told us that we were going to be the biggest thing since sliced bread and we hung on his every word. That was even the case on the regular occasions we found ourselves penniless and had to go and ask him for money. Milton's answer would be to line up on his desk shots of Bacardi for each of us. By the time the meeting had finished, we would have agreed to everything that he said and felt extremely happy to be leaving his office with a fiver apiece. I never did get so much as a royalty payment out of Beacon, even after our first single was a Top 10 hit in Germany.

At the beginning of 1970, we went in to make the *UFO 1* record. The studio we used was in a small town called Rickmansworth in Hertfordshire, right out in the sticks, and only had a little four-track desk. Our two producers, Guy Fletcher and Doug Flett, were both also songwriters and had written for the Hollies and Cliff Richard. In fact, the pair of them went on to write Cliff's Eurovision Song Contest entry for 1973. That was a song called 'Power to All Our Friends', which reached the dizzy heights of third in the competition. We recorded in the evening, since the four of us in the band still had day jobs. I hadn't passed my driving test, so had to rely on a lift from a friend, but then the whole process only took a week. We had a shoestring budget, so couldn't afford the luxury of any longer. Like Blue Cheer had done, we cut an Eddie Cochran song, 'C'mon Everybody', and also a catchy little number of our own that grew out of a very simple, chugging riff that Mick hit upon. Dum-dum-dam, dum-dum-dam it went, and that became 'Boogie for George', our debut single and German smash. Most of the songs evolved in the same way, with one of us coming up with an initial idea and the others jamming along with it.

I haven't a clue as to why, but the French as well as the Germans latched on to 'Boogie for George'. Wholly unexpectedly, our album took off right across Europe just as soon as it was released that October. That gave us the opportunity to cross the Channel and be able to play to a couple of thousand people a night, which was a bit of a shock to the system. Up until then, we had not been in front of more than a handful of people at home. We played every major city and town in Germany and France, but also in Italy, Luxembourg and Switzerland. We were still only getting paid around £50 a week, but that was fine by me just so long as people turned up to see us.

Germany especially was like being in a different world. We were treated like pop stars all of a sudden and people wanted our autographs. None of us had experienced anything like that at home, and then there were the German girls. It wasn't so much a case of us chasing the German girls as of being besieged by them. I was astonished by that, but also by the fact that they would do things that their English counterparts wouldn't even contemplate. Literally, they were up for anything. Before you knew it, the German girls would be topless, bottomless, and whatever hotel we were staying in would end up being more like a brothel. And all that any of them seemed to want to do was have sex with the band – any one of us, or even all of us at the same time.

Of course, I was going steady with Yvonne by then but felt helpless to resist. My life at home was nice but staid, sometimes boring even, and this was anything but dull. We were back and forth to Germany for the next year or so, and I had my own harem every night. There were also two nurses who followed us around the country and kept us supplied with Mandrax hot off the production line. They weren't the best-looking girls and just wanted to hang out with the band, so we plied them with booze and reserved the Randy Mandy's for the more attractive fräuleins. Bloody hell, for a young lad it was truly unbelievable what went on.

Neill Way: I don't think Pete ever grew up. I remember one particular occasion during the early days of him going off to Europe with the band and when he was back home for a spell in the summer. He used to cycle a lot at the time and rode off one morning from Enfield intending to cash a cheque at the bank in Kentish Town. He came off his bike, though, and never made it as far as the bank. He had to call Mum and plead with her to go and meet him at the tube station, because he didn't have the money for a train ticket. When Mum got to the station, she explained to the ticket collector that she meant to take care of her son's fare when he got off the train. This guy smiled at her and said, 'That's the trouble with the school holidays, love, all these bloody helpless kids on the loose.' Mum had to explain to him that her helpless kid was actually a grown man of twenty.

Those first German tours lifted my ego and not just because I got to have so much sex. Through all of the girls and also the crowds that came to see us, I could see we had something going as a band and that was worth pursuing. However, there was a downside to all of the fun. Whenever I got back home, I would have to go for a check-up at the venereal disease clinic in Holloway. Inevitably, quite often I found out that

I had returned with NSU, gonorrhoea or something equally nasty, and that would make things very difficult with Yvonne. We would have been apart for weeks, but I would have to pretend I was too tired for sex and hope that the penicillin I'd been prescribed would work fast. We had a band code for such a circumstance, 'THTH', or 'Too Hot to Handle', which later became the title of one of our best-known songs. However, it must have been obvious to Yvonne that something wasn't quite right.

Towards the end of 1970, we went over to Japan for the first time. We were put up in an apartment in Tokyo and one night ran into Jimmy Page, John Bonham and Led Zeppelin's manager, Peter Grant, at a club. They were in town to do the local football stadium and sat at the next table to us. We got talking to them for what seemed like hours. They were very nice; I think Jimmy was quite impressed by the fact I'd seen the New Yardbirds at the Marquee. I couldn't hear enough of what they had to say, even if it was just small talk. Zeppelin was the band I measured us against and most aspired to be like.

The girls in Japan were crackers, too. Every night of our stay, there would be three hundred or so camped outside of our apartment, each of them as young and beautiful as those in Germany. One night, I did acid with a bunch of them and got whisked off to a village on the coast. To this day I've no idea what it was called or even where it is precisely, but there were houses on stilts in the middle of the sea and it felt to me like being at the end of the world, especially as I was tripping at the time. I also ended up knocking off the American ambassador to Japan's daughter. She came along to one of our shows. I never did get her name, but she was bloody good in bed, I know that, and had the scratches to prove it. The thing was, though, that all of these experiences soon began to merge into one. They were there and then gone.

Like Zeppelin, we were also booked to do an outdoor show in Tokyo, at Hibiya Park in front of 23,000 people. However, the evening of the gig was so humid that a cut on my left index finger started to open up and it got to be too painful for me to play. We were forced to cut short our set, which incited a bit of a riot. Part of our *Live in Japan* album of 1971 was recorded that night and on that record you can actually hear the trouble kick off. Initially, I was taken aback that people would want to see us *that* much, but we ended up with a price to pay. The park is sited right next to the Emperor's palace and our promoter was liable for any damages. We had been driven into Tokyo like heroes in a limousine, but left as villains and crammed in the back of a taxi.

The most disorientating thing about my new life was that when I went back to England, we were nobodies again. *UFO 1* had made no impression at all on the British charts, so the only place of note that we were able to play at home was the Marquee Club. The guy who owned the Marquee was a colourful character named Jack Barry. He was an older man and had a family, but was gay, notoriously predatory and quite happy to have young boys hang about the place. On one occasion, Jack tried to seduce me down in the club's cellar. He referred to it as his office, but it was where he kept his beer and had his private assignations. On this particular night, Jack asked me to accompany him to the office. I thought he was going to offer me drugs, and would give anything a go once, but soon enough he made it clear what he actually had in mind.

There was an awkward silence between us and then I told him to leave it out. Jack never mentioned the incident again.

To be honest, people would often think I *was* gay. A few years later, we were rehearsing for a tour out at Shepperton Studios and Elton John was working there at the same time. A former roadie of ours had gone on to be Elton's tour manager and, one afternoon, he asked me if I'd like to go and watch Elton run through his solo piano show. I thought it was an open invitation to me and anyone else who fancied turning up, so gratefully accepted. At the appointed hour, I was led into a large, hangar-like room. There was Elton, sat at a grand piano and lit by a single spotlight. He was in the midst of playing 'Candle in the Wind'. It was only after fifteen or so minutes that I realized that, other than Elton, I was the only other person in the room. It occurred to me then that Elton might think I was gay and had granted me a special personal performance, so to speak. He had not actually spoken a word to me, but had simply carried on running through one hit after another. To be polite, I listened to him do three or four more songs and then sort of shuffled back to the boys.

With all of the touring that the band was doing, Yvonne and I hadn't got to see too much of each other. Nevertheless, we decided to get married. We weren't even living together at the time and I was just twenty. It was a traditional white wedding and afterwards we rented a house in the East End, where Yvonne had been brought up. The two of us had some good times there, and also a child together, a daughter named Zowie. By then, my salary had doubled to £100 a week. If I'd had a normal job, we may well have had a future together.

Neill Way: The wedding was at Saint Matthew's Church, Bethnal Green. It was a big old affair and Phil, Mick and Andy were all in attendance. This was just after they had returned from Japan and were starting to break into the big league. Yvonne was a typical East End girl, very nice and friendly. The trouble was that no sooner was Pete home than he'd be back out on tour again, and quite often wouldn't actually forewarn her of his going. There were several occasions when Pete told Yvonne he was just popping down the shop for a pint of milk and would then be off for a month or more.

———

We started work on our second record, *Flying*, almost exactly a year to the day since we had begun the first. Once again, we used Guy and Doug as producers but this time we were more conveniently based in central London, at Nova Studios just off Oxford Street. The rise in salary from the band had allowed me to give up my day job, but it was another of Beacon's in-and-out affairs. Each of us contributed to the songwriting and we had quite grand ambitions for the album. As a band, we were acutely aware of how rock music was evolving and specifically of what the likes of Zeppelin and Sabbath were up to. We wanted to achieve what they had, and in 1971 Zeppelin had progressed to conjuring up 'Stairway to Heaven' and the rest of their classic *IV* album. That was the gauntlet that had been laid down for us, and as such we came up with a couple of epic songs of our own for *Flying*: the title track, and 'Star Storm', which each ran to twenty minutes or more. We meant to create more of an atmosphere than actual songs, since that appeared to be the mood of the time, but truth be told, I don't think our efforts have aged particularly well. At best, they sound naïve now and, at worst, a load of old rubbish.

Unfortunately, Mick had also started to hold us back. He was a great player, but had begun to get very introverted to the point it became obvious he no longer enjoyed being in the band. He had not long got engaged to be married and the problem was he didn't want to have to keep going away from home. It was a hard slog for all of us, but if you can't have fun there's really no point in being in a band. In the end, it was better all round for Mick to leave.

Not that his replacement was any better suited to UFO. Larry Wallis was one of the local in-crowd and a hippy. He liked nothing more than to smoke a joint and would have been better off in bloody Hawkwind, though he later joined an early version of Motörhead. We got on well enough with him and had a laugh, but the band just didn't sound very good with Larry on guitar. He wanted to be the next Jeff Beck, which would have been fine had he actually sounded anything like Beck. Half the time, though, he would play in a completely different key to the rest of us.

To add to my misery, it was just as we were due to go out on tour in Europe with Larry that the breakdown in my marriage truly started. Sadly for me, Yvonne just didn't share my vision of what our life together was going to end up being. I would be gone from home for six weeks at a time and she had a very good idea of what I would be getting up to while I was away. She was, I think, just waiting for me to stop messing around with music and go back to having a proper job. Where, though, would I rather be? Going off to Germany, France or Italy and my harems of girls, or sat around at home waiting to go into an office every morning? Every tour for me was like being spirited off on a magical schoolboy outing, so of course there was no contest.

On this occasion, I was supposed to meet up with the band at King's Cross and drive down to Germany. However, Yvonne was adamant that I should not go and we had a huge bust-up. In fact, she locked me in our bedroom and tried to set fire to my passport. I gave her half an hour to calm down and then managed to convince her to let me out of the bedroom. I told her that of course I would stay at home, and then pulled my usual trick, which was to plead that I just wanted to pop down the road for a newspaper. Somehow or other, I snuck my bag out with me and met up with the band as scheduled. I did at least call Yvonne when we finally arrived in Germany, but not surprisingly she was still enraged. That was the thing, though: rock and roll meant everything to me and I just couldn't give it up.

However, despite countless hours in rehearsal, Larry had not improved the band and the gigs didn't go too well. We even got booed off at a couple of shows, so enough was enough. The next guy to come in and audition was Bernie Marsden, who was more like Mick Bolton as a character, easy-going and very down to earth, but could actually play like Paul Kossoff. Bernie gave us some much-needed stability, but at the same time there was still nothing about us as a band that was out of the ordinary. Fortune, however, was about to smile upon us. For our next European tour we had a young German band called the Scorpions open for us. Their lead guitarist was a teenage whizz-kid named Michael Schenker, who looked great and played even better. Phil and I would watch the Scorpions from the side of the stage and the difference between their band and ours was obvious. Michael was amazing, a virtuoso, but also an odd combination of very shy and outgoing at the same time. It wasn't until later that we found out that his personality would be dependent on the amount of beer he had drunk.

A happy accident apparently occurred when we were due to play a show at Nuremberg University. Bernie lost his passport and wasn't able to travel. At least, Bernie claimed to have lost his passport. I suspect the truth was that the rest of us had by then driven Bernie round the bend. Later on, of course, he had great success as a member of David Coverdale's Whitesnake. David once told me he had pressed Bernie on what it was like being in UFO. According to him, Bernie just shook his head and said, 'It was like you wouldn't believe.'

At all events, the Nuremberg gig had sold out and the promoter pleaded with us to go ahead with the show. In those days, audiences would smash up the building if a band didn't play. Michael's elder brother, Rudolph, was the Scorpions' bandleader and Phil and I went to ask him if we could borrow Michael for a short set. Luckily, Michael knew a few of our songs because they had been on German radio. The first time the two of us actually played together was in the gents' toilet at the university. I had to run through the chord changes with him, the two of us sat side by side on the loo, which was doubly tricky since he didn't speak a word of English at the time and the only German I knew was, 'Ein bier, bitte'.

We only played for forty-five minutes, but went down well that night and also the next when Bernie still hadn't turned up. There was clearly a greater chemistry between Michael and Phil, Andy and me. I wouldn't say fun was the optimum word to describe it, but there were no rules and it was so much more exciting. Bernie did eventually arrive on the scene, but the ensuing shows with him were almost an anti-climax. We were, though, saved from a tricky conversation at the end of the tour by the fact that Bernie had in any case decided to go off and join another band called Wild Turkey.

Michael basically joined our band for the rest of the tour, even though he was also still a member of the Scorpions. Quite often on the afternoon before a show, the two bands would play each other at football and Michael would turn out for us at centre forward. He was good, too: a star striker. After the gigs, he would come back to the hotel with us rather than them, although he never actually stayed in the room he booked. Every night, he would instead go off with a different girl and sleep at her house. However, next morning he would be back at the hotel at 10 a.m. prompt for the bus to the next city, still in his stage clothes. For my part, I was by then virtually living on Mandrax. I'd do a handful of pills, around seven or eight, before each show. That stuff was fantastic for knocking you out, but you had to be spot on with your timing. One night, I took my dose a little too early and consequently passed out onstage during the last song of the encore. I was literally out cold and had to be carried off. After every gig, we would also ferry a car full of girls back to the hotel. As we were being driven, we would fuck them on the back seat and lean out of the windows and shout at the pedestrians. It had become the accepted thing for us to share, so once we were at the hotel, the girls would then be passed between us from one room to another.

Each morning, I would wake up, surrounded by nymphs, drink a bottle of wine for breakfast and then travel on to the next show, while waving out of the bus window, like a flag, the bed-sheet from the night before, which would be covered in blood from a girl being on her period. I thought the whole experience absolutely mind-blowing, but then who wouldn't? After all, this was everything that I had worked for and then some.

At the end of the tour, Michael conveyed to Phil and me, through his steady girlfriend, that he wanted us to tell Rudolph he meant to leave the Scorpions and move to London with UFO. At that point, I didn't have any sense that Michael was, well, liable to go bananas. After our summit with Rudolph, though, we were left with the distinct impression that he and the Scorpions' singer, Klaus Meine, went off clapping their hands and saying to each other, 'Jah, those stupid Engländers have taken him off our hands!'

CHAPTER 4

Arriving in the Land of the Free, the wide-eyed young rocker is met with open arms and an inexhaustible supply of Peruvian marching powder.

───────

By the time Michael officially joined the band, we found ourselves between record deals. Beacon Records had folded, in what to us were mysterious circumstances and which Milton Samuels didn't bother to explain. Our money got stopped, though, which was a sure-fire sign that something was up. Obviously, our sales in Germany hadn't helped Milton that much. We had, though, begun courting another label, Chrysalis, and so we went off with Michael to record a demo for them at Rockfield Studios in Wales. Our contact at Chrysalis was Wilf Wright, who worked for their management arm and in that capacity looked after both Robin Trower and Supertramp. Whenever I went to Chrysalis's offices, Roger Hodgson of Supertramp would also be sat outside waiting to see Wilf. That was the thing about Wilf: he never failed to appear busy. Roger and

I used to swear that he had a button hidden under his desk, because no sooner had you finally got in to see him than his phone would ring and he'd excuse himself.

Michael was at the time lodging with Phil in Tottenham. He was quite easy-going in those days, perhaps because he didn't yet appreciate our humour. The funny thing was, the more English he picked up the harder it was for us to understand him. But with Michael in the band we at last started to pull in crowds at home. We broke the attendance record at the Marquee and trekked up to play at such faraway places as Cleethorpes and Newcastle and were surprised to find the clubs full.

Neill Way: I'd certainly got to know Phil and Andy, but it was Michael that I got on best with when he joined the band. After living a while at Phil's, Michael started to rent a flat in Winchmore Hill, which was not far from where I lived with Mum and Dad. Occasionally, I'd go round to his place of an evening and sit there while he worked out different things on his guitar. He seemed welded to his guitar and was never without it. Generally, the other three were always fooling around or pulling pranks on each other. Phil could be pretty serious but was a nice enough guy, while Andy was the butt of all jokes. Pete would often invite me down to see the band at the Marquee and tell me that he would put my name on the guest-list. Well, the number of times I was stood at the door of the Marquee having to explain who I was because he'd forgotten to do it.

Michael Schenker: For me, it was just about the music. When I joined UFO, I didn't look to form great friendships but was instead focused on playing my guitar and discovering my art and self-expression. It didn't even matter to me who the band was – I just wanted to be in Britain, because that was where all the artists that I loved had come from. I was blessed, though, with the individuals in that band and particularly with Pete. Somehow or other, we had an incredible presence. Pete was never what you would call technical on the bass, but I found the way he played to be tasteful and certainly all heart. He's a guy who doesn't play on his own, never practises. He needs to be out in front of people and to be watched.

I don't want to glorify all the sex, drugs and rock-and-roll stuff. Pete and I started off together as kids and did the same things as everybody else at that time. There were girls, drugs and alcohol, and it was nothing special. We had our good and bad times, but Pete always was the charmer. He was very loving, friendly and positive and talked a lot about nothing. There was never silence with Pete. He had to talk all the time. Luckily for me, I didn't speak any English so it went in one ear and out the other. There was a lot of cynical stuff that went on in the band. I guess sarcasm is a big part of the English sense of humour. On one later occasion, Andy Parker told me that if I had known what Pete and Phil were saying at that time I would not have stayed in the band.

Eventually, we signed to Chrysalis and at that point Wilf Wright also took over as our manager. We didn't have a falling out as such with Terry Collins and Johnny Spence, but our relationship with them had clearly run its course and Wilf seemed to us to be in a different league. I mean to say, he had been road manager for both Led Zeppelin and Black Sabbath and that alone was good enough for me. Not that the deal we got from Chrysalis was so great. In effect, they would pay us quite a low royalty rate, and at the same time we would have to borrow high expenses off them to tour. That ended up hitting all of us hard, but right then we were happy just to have another record label.

Our third album, *Phenomenon*, was written at a little rehearsal place under the tube station in Walthamstow. It was hardly glamorous, but it was apparent to all of us from the start that the record would be a big step up for the band. Michael had a lot of guitar melodies knocking about, which we demoed on his Revox tape machine – a lot of that record sounds almost acoustic because of the way it was put together. Some of Michael's ideas were quite basic, but also very immediate and impactful. His soloing was a different matter and often as not would take your breath away. Phil would chip in with choruses and lyrics, but otherwise sat and read the paper. It was pretty much a process of trial and error, but two of our best-loved songs came out of those writing sessions – 'Rock Bottom' and 'Doctor Doctor'. Both are now, of course, held up as rock classics, but I don't think 'Doctor Doctor' sold more than ten copies when we first put it out as a single in the UK. Musically, Michael fitted in perfectly and gave us a broader scope, but Phil, Andy and I had also been playing together for three or four years by then, so as a band we were like a well-oiled machine. We recorded the album at Morgan Studios in Willesden, north London, which Zeppelin, Pink Floyd and the Kinks had all used in the recent past. We had a new producer as well, Leo Lyons, who was also the bassist with blues-rockers Ten Years After. That band was renowned for Alvin Lee's long guitar solos, so Leo was quite happy to let Michael have a free rein, which worked to our considerable advantage. The whole band, though, was fired up and Leo essentially just recorded us the way we sounded in our rehearsal room. In that sense, it's a very honest, accurate album.

Joe Elliott, Def Leppard vocalist: I first discovered UFO at sixteen and in the week that I went to work at Osborne's steel factory in Sheffield. There was another lad who started at Osborne's the same day as me, Colin Woodcock. The two of us got talking together about music. I browbeat Colin about the American band Montrose and he introduced me to UFO. Colin lent me his copy of Phenomenon *and the second I heard 'Doctor Doctor', I was hooked. Everything about that record was great, but I was particularly struck by just how different UFO sounded to other great British rock bands of the time like Zeppelin or Sabbath. They weren't like Bowie, Marc Bolan or the Sweet either, who were also huge at the time, but I guess they fit somewhere in between all of them and in a place of their own.*

To begin with at least, *Phenomenon* didn't sell as well as Chrysalis had expected, but they still sent us off to America for the first time and that's when the madness really started. We flew out to Seattle and then on to San Francisco, where we did our first club show. The next stop was Los Angeles. We were billeted at the infamous Hyatt House on Sunset Strip, which Zeppelin and pretty much every other major rock act of the era used to frequent. The hotel was more often referred to as the Riot House and that name was entirely accurate. Strewn about the place at all times of night and day were all these stunningly attractive girls with next to nothing on.

Once again, Phil and I had to share a room, and the very second we walked through the door, the phone rang. It was a girl and she asked if she and her friends could come over and have fun with us. God knows how, or even if, she knew who we were, but who was I to say no? From that moment on, the party didn't stop and that entire trip turned out to be all that I had fantasized about as a budding teenage rock star and more. The American girls were so uninhibited they made even the Germans look like nuns. They were a further notch up in the looks department, too, every one of them like a catwalk model. Throw in the drugs and the whole of that first US tour ended up being absolute insanity, though that for me was soon par for the course. It didn't take any of us long to slip into 'anything goes' mode, and in that respect, Wilf was the main instigator. Wilf was very serious and business-like when the occasion demanded it, but a different side to him emerged on the road. I suppose he had started off by going on tour with Ozzy Osbourne; anyway, he was like a man possessed.

Of course, the most important thing to us as a band was to make a good impression on American audiences. For every British rock act, America was like the Holy Land, the place that mattered most, and taking it by storm as Zeppelin had done was our biggest goal. On that first visit, we opened up for all kinds of other bands: Steppenwolf, Jethro Tull, Foghat, REO Speedwagon, Rod Stewart and the Faces, and more. In general, we didn't have much to do with the headline acts. They wouldn't turn up until it was time for them to go on and then they'd progress straight from a fleet of limos to the stage. That fact in itself was an inspiration for us to go on and make a name for ourselves. We did two nights with Rod and the Faces at Cobo Hall in Detroit. An 18,000-seat arena, it was almost deserted both nights when we went on. I looked up at the empty balconies and, beyond them, could see the hot dog and beer stands on the concourses swarming with people. The place was packed by the time the Faces came out, though, and there was an absolute riot. Literally, they had to have riot police on the floor to try and control the crowd, who let off fireworks. Talk about making you feel insignificant and small, but we got an education that night in how to be flash but also exude class and total confidence.

We had an even harder time with other bands. REO Speedwagon, for instance, insisted that we should not be allowed backstage at the same time as them. They had their wives and children with them and claimed we were too dangerous for them to be around. In the first instance, I think it was the fact that we'd had a water pistol fight that had annoyed them. That and also perhaps because we would do fistfuls of Quaaludes after a show and then stagger around the place like zombies. I didn't like them or their music anyway; it was like watered-down rock. It was the same with Styx, another American band we played with in those early days. They were a dreadful, humourless bunch and full of themselves, too. As such, we preferred to keep to ourselves and our drugs.

Back then, I hadn't been properly introduced to cocaine so I remember being tired most of the time. I would invariably pick up a girl to take back to the hotel after a show and never get enough sleep. Even more debilitating, in America especially we had to fly everywhere, and that was a particular nightmare for me. I hated flying, was terrified of it. I was forever expecting an engine to fail and for us to plummet out of the sky. I didn't know that a plane could fly on one engine, and we had to go through some of the worst weather in the American winter. I honestly think that was one of the main causes of me becoming an alcoholic. I was in a perpetually paranoid state, but so long as there was a bar on the plane I could numb myself with vats of booze.

———

Unfortunately, it was our going off to America that hastened the end of my marriage. It had been a drawn-out process, but Yvonne and I had drifted apart because I was hardly at home. I'm not sure any marriage could have endured my lifestyle at that point. I wasn't really a husband in any conventional sense and I couldn't blame Yvonne for getting fed up of being left on her own with Zowie. Plus, I was seeing other women; then Yvonne found someone else, too, and that was the end of that. By the time I got home from the tour, Yvonne had moved out of the house.

In the couple of years that followed I did see Zowie, but not often. I was out of the country a lot of the time and didn't know where she was living with Yvonne. There was always so much going on in my life that I wasn't able to keep track of theirs, nor did I want to interfere. Yvonne had wanted to bring Zowie up in a normal, stable environment, so in her wisdom looked for and apparently found someone who was the complete opposite of me. Of course, I very much missed seeing my daughter grow up and it's quite possible that Yvonne and I would still be together now if I hadn't chosen the band over her. Boyfriend and girlfriend tended to get married for keeps back in those days and it was all very local. The problem was that I became international. And no sooner had we got back from the States than we were off on a European tour, so there was never the time to stop and properly consider anything or anyone else. I threw myself back into my work instead, and that would always be the case. It had become apparent that the new songs needed an extra element to boost them on stage, so we decided to hire a rhythm guitarist for this next batch of dates and to fill out the holes in our live sound. We held auditions and the outstanding candidate was a Welsh guy, Paul Chapman, who had been playing with an Irish band, Skid Row, and had replaced the very well-regarded Gary Moore in their line-up. Paul set out his stall straight away, reeling down the road to rehearsals clutching a half-empty bottle of cider. Michael was quite happy with the arrangement, too, so much so that the two of them ended up sharing a lot of the lead parts.

There was one show in Germany on that tour that I vividly remember, but not for the gig itself. It took place in a sports hall and, afterwards, Andy was doing the dirty deed with a young girl in our dressing room. Several other people were also waiting their turn, but it was to Andy's particular surprise that the caretaker of the building all of a sudden appeared. This guy was keen to close up for the night and commenced to prod Andy's naked bum with the point of his finger. Somewhat aggrieved, Andy shrieked, 'Oi, gerroff!' and went back to the task at hand and indeed managed to finish his business.

After that, Michael quite literally carried this same girl back to our hotel, whereupon we discovered that we had forgotten to collect a night key and were locked out. It was the middle of winter; snow was on the ground and cold enough to freeze a brass monkey's balls. As the rest of us attempted to break back into the hotel, Michael stood there like Frankenstein's monster, cradling this poor, naked girl in his arms. When we finally succeeded in our mission, nature duly took its course between the two of them. And that was by no means a one-off series of events.

It was our next album, *Force It*, which really opened the door for us in America. That was a very natural-sounding record and a favourite of mine. Michael came up with some truly great riffs and I co-wrote a couple of songs that would go on to become staples of our live sets, 'Shoot Shoot' and 'Out in the Street'. There was something quite evocative about Phil's words to 'Out in the Street' and also to another of that album's best songs, 'Mother Mary'. He would often surprise me with his lyrics, which also I think set the band apart. There were no great philosophies in what Phil wrote, but he avoided the usual rock-and-roll clichés and was able to paint a picture in words. I put that down to the fact that he read a lot of books, or so it seemed to me.

Force It was the first album of ours to chart in the US. In part, at least, that was perhaps helped by its cover artwork. As we had done with *Phenomenon*, we were able to use the Hipgnosis design team who were responsible for all of those classic Pink Floyd album covers, like *Dark Side of the Moon* and *Wish You Were Here*. Hipgnosis came up with something just as distinctive for us. A pun on the American word for tap, faucet, it was a photograph of an attractive young couple, well, fucking in the shower. You couldn't have missed it in a record shop, that was for sure.

Pete Makowski, then working as a writer for the weekly British music paper Sounds: *The first time I met Pete was just before* Force It *came out in summer 1975. I remember it being a very awkward interview to do. I was sat at one end of a table in Chrysalis's London office, Pete and Phil Mogg at the other, and neither of them was very forthcoming. They were both aloof, but Pete was particularly quiet.*

61

The thing that struck me most about them was the way that they were dressed. They looked like a band that had toured Germany a lot, with really tight trousers and shag haircuts. The only time Pete lit up during the whole interview was when he talked about going to see gigs at Camden Roundhouse. He told me how he would get ampoules of Methedrine, break them into orange juice, and then be up all night.

The thing about Pete is that away from the band thing he's quite shy and also very insecure. In that respect, he was very similar to Ozzy Osbourne. I interviewed Ozzy in the early days of his solo career and he really didn't have too much of a personality. It was only when people started to write more about his antics that he became this sort of cartoon character. Pete was the same.

Ross Halfin, rock photographer: *I suppose UFO did dress a little bit like women back then, but compared to all the glam bands that were around at the time they had a real sort of blokey edge which made them stand out. The only other up-and-coming thing you had going on at the time was pub rock, and I particularly hated Dr Feelgood and their ilk. That was a dreadful scene, whereas UFO was more of a classic British rock band. I ended up working with them for many years and they were also a quintessentially London band, which I really liked about them.*

I was in Los Angeles for the start of the *Force It* tour when an executive from Chrysalis asked me if I'd rather have a steak lunch or a line of coke. Everyone in the American music business appeared to be taking cocaine at the time. As a drug, there was something especially attractive about it. Coke appeared to make you feel confident and if you knew how to get hold of the good stuff, girls would be around it like bees to honey. So that was an easy enough choice for me to make and

I liked it from that very first moment I took it. My cocaine use pretty much spiralled from then on. It raised my spirits and I found myself in lots of interesting situations with very famous people because of the fact we all took coke. When it wasn't about, I felt somehow lesser, reduced in stature and personality. Fortunately, coke could be found *everywhere* in America and I got particularly adept at identifying drug dealers who would want to go out on the road with us.

Upon arrival in a new town, the first thing I would do was establish who the guy was who could bring 'x' amount of coke straight to our hotel. It would be a great tragedy if no one was about, but a rare occurrence. There were so many dealers that I have trouble now recalling all of their faces, let alone their names. Back then, I made it a point, though, not to do coke before we went on stage. You get an energy lapse immediately after taking it and I wanted the show to be as good as possible, perfect even. In that respect, at least, I had a certain amount of discipline. However, once I came off stage, feeling exhausted, there was nothing better than a line or two of Peruvian marching powder to perk me up.

I've thought quite a lot since about why I had such an insatiable appetite for drugs and have come to the conclusion I was born with an addictive personality. As a kid, it was running that I got obsessed by and I'd run all the time, every day. That was also my first taste of adulation – the heady acclaim I got from coming second for my club in a cross-country race. It's true also that by nature I'm quite a shy person, but I don't believe I've ever done drugs to compensate for that. It was more the case that they seemed to give me a lift, particularly coke along with a couple of drinks.

Truthfully, I've never done drugs, or drank to excess, in order to cultivate a rock-and-roll image or to make people think I was over the top. Since I was around drugs from my early teens, I just thought of taking them as everyday behaviour. To me, the whole point of doing my job was to put on a good show, but the reward was being able to have a bottle of Jack Daniel's and a couple of lines of coke. That started off with a guy offering me a line and progressed to dealers who had thousands of dollars of the stuff on them.

It was also in America that I was truly made aware of just how excited people would get that I was in a band – and most especially an English band. All sorts of people would want to hang out with me because I was a musician, and the easiest way for them to buy their way into our entourage was to have drugs. In that respect, LA was the best city of all. If I had time off in LA, I'd take a car down to the Whiskey A Go Go or Starwood on Sunset Strip. Generally, I would get free drinks all night at both clubs and could rely on the fact that someone or other would come over to my table to offer me a livener. It was a very sociable environment and I met a lot of friends that I didn't know I'd got. Being young and English, I really had my pick of the girls as well. The LA girls were always dressed to the nines and expert at chatting you up. The name of your band, where you were from and where you were staying, that was the crucial information for them to establish. It was a mesmerizing ritual and I was like a lamb to the slaughter. I got to sleep with more women than I could possibly count, hundreds at least, and in every permutation you can imagine. It was as if I were starring in my own graphic porn movie. Regularly, I'd have two, three or more girls at a time, and if I ever got tired, or just wanted to sit there and do drugs, they would give me a blowjob, or else entertain me by having sex with each other or by themselves. These were girls from well-to-do backgrounds, too, but there was nothing they wouldn't do. And right then, the fact I had sex on tap, and in any position I could dream up, was beyond my wildest imagination. By the time I was into my thirties and then forties, though, it wasn't quite so exciting to be sat in a hotel room watching two girls fuck each other for my pleasure.

In truth, we were all of us taking advantage of each other. I mean to say, the girls got what they wanted out of the arrangement, too. In LA, every one of them looked as if she should be auditioning for parts in Hollywood movies. And they had reasoned that the best way for them to get to know someone famous was to be involved with a guy in a band. As a group, they would travel here, there and everywhere to be with us, and there were no questions asked. If they looked old enough, they were. And they knew the procedure. It was in and out. None of the girls ever had any money on them, and having to get them taxis home in the middle of the night used to put a huge dent in my wallet. Each of them would profess undying love for me, and then be off fucking someone like Steven Tyler of Aerosmith the next night.

San Francisco was the same as LA. As soon as you touched down on the ground, if you were an English band – wham! And it didn't matter to the girls how famous you were. In fact, being less well known seemed to make you more of a target, as if they were staking their claim to you early on. Eventually, though, it reached the point where I had a more regular girl in every major city in the States, which made my life a little easier. I'm sure it all sounds very immoral, but what can I tell you? It does get to be a bit boring when it's just four blokes sat around all day waiting to play. And so long as you kept in mind that none of these girls were hanging on to your every word because you were the man of their dreams, then it was all just good, clean fun.

Not that we didn't have other diversions. Phil and I, in particular, shared a room so often that we fell into a routine of talking about the other members of the band. Well, we had to have something other than drinking to do. Andy, in particular, was under high observation and often as not the hapless victim of our endless scheming. We would do daft things like put fish in his shoes and institute secret code words for him. Phil used to insist that Andy had no neck, so between the two of us he became 'NNL', or the No-Neck Look. One time we had a day off in Buffalo and were staying at the local Holiday Inn. We persuaded the girl on the front desk to put a sign up for us on the display board outside of the hotel that read: 'Welcome Andy Lout and the NNL Party'. Andy went fucking berserk when he saw it.

Andy had a good sense of humour, but you wouldn't want to cross the line with him. He would get this look in his eyes that Phil and I christened the 'Red Light'. Truthfully, Andy was and is very serious about his craft, which perhaps we didn't appreciate at the time. That night in Buffalo, ten of us had to take him off to a strip club just to calm him down. Even then, things went wrong. A member of our party who shall remain nameless tried to touch one of the girls while she was dancing. One minute he was there, the next he was being frog-marched off the premises by two giant security guards.

It was different with Michael. Phil and I would never, ever take the piss out of Michael, or at least not to his face. 'Don't bring out the Führer' – that became our private motto. Don't get me wrong, Michael liked to have a laugh but he's the sort of person who would be very offended if he thought you were having fun at his expense. Of course, he also hadn't grown up with us and wasn't even from the same country. Michael was focused on his guitar and didn't appreciate distractions. That being said, he did carry a ventriloquist's dummy around with him for several weeks at one point. I never did find out why. By then, though, we had started to become aware of his eccentricities. It wouldn't be too long before we also grew accustomed to worrying about what he might do next.

On that tour, we made our first appearance on American television, which was another rung up the ladder. We were invited to appear on *Don Kirshner's Rock Concert*, a big deal at the time. Kirshner's show was syndicated nationwide and pretty much every major act in America got to record a show for it, including the Eagles, Sabbath, Bowie, Kiss and Alice Cooper. We shot our episode before a live studio audience in Long Beach, California. It went out later on that same Saturday evening and made quite an impact; we were firing on all cylinders that night and lots of musicians and fans in America have since told me that it was then that they first became aware of UFO. Actually, I managed to miss our historic broadcast. Backstage after the filming, somebody had handed me what I thought was a joint but turned out to be THC, a horse tranquilizer. I smoked it in the men's room with the girl I'd picked up for the night. It knocked both of us out and we ended up having to be stretchered back to the Riot House.

Even forty-eight hours later I was still finding it difficult to walk and talk.

At the same time, Lemmy was also resident at the Riot House and on the lookout for people to hang out with because he was on his own. This was right after he'd got himself kicked out of Hawkwind for getting busted on the Canadian border for possession of speed. After the THC had finally worn off, Lemmy went out and bought me a record – 'Psychotic Reaction' by the Count Five. From then on, I always got on very well with Lemmy. I thought of him as one of life's great philosophers and a natural born leader. He was the sort of guy who wouldn't be told what to do, and he was also in love with rock and roll to the extent that he'd built his whole life around it.

The fondest memories I have of Lemmy are of the two of us having a drink together and him holding court on the meaning of life. He would also lecture me, though, especially later on when I started doing heroin. He would say to me, 'You should give that stuff up, Peter' – he always called me Peter – 'and just take speed instead.' It was like getting advice from a doctor. But I don't recall a bad word ever passing between us.

I never saw Lemmy drunk. He could drink Jack Daniel's all day and it appeared to pass through his system without having any noticeable effect. His digestive system seemed to have perfectly adapted to his lifestyle. In my experience, Lemmy never changed in that respect or indeed any other. Well, he might have changed his jeans just the once, but you would venture into his hotel room at your peril because of the lethal smell of his socks.

PART TWO:

Flying

CHAPTER 5

*A collective move to the fair city of Los Angeles
is undertaken, and fortune and a senator's wife
smile upon our errant hero.*

———

I met Josephine through a mutual friend at the record company in London. She was lodging at his flat in Ealing at the time and I went round to see him when I got back from the *Force It* tour. The two of them were on their way out for a meal when I arrived and she invited me along. I didn't need to be asked twice. I'm sure I sound like a broken record, but Jo was a knockout brunette. In normal circumstances, I wouldn't have been able to take my eyes off her the whole night. The thing was, though, I had dashed out and had no idea how much cash I'd got on me. As a result, I spent the entire meal fretting instead about whether I'd have enough to pay my share of the bill. I did just about manage it, but with only a couple of quid to spare.

After that night, though, Jo and I were rarely apart, at least when I wasn't on the road. It was just one of those things where we hit it off straight away. It was a different kind of relationship to the one I'd had with Yvonne, more grown-up, I guess you could say. The two of us ate out a lot, she shared my love of music, and it wasn't long before we moved in together. We found a place to rent in a pre-war mansion block just off from Abbey Road. It had a walled garden and was a minute's walk from the famous recording studios.

I enjoyed making Jo laugh and we grew very close, very quickly, like soulmates, even though we did have quite different personalities. Then again, I don't know that there is anyone who is the same as me. Jo was straightforward and could be blunt, whereas I was more of a dreamer and impulsive. There were times when she treated me as if I were the Devil, but I couldn't blame her, since I carried on with all of the aspects of my rock-and-roll life. She did, though, change me in other respects. It was because of Jo that I became a vegetarian, which I still am to this day. Apart, that is, for the occasional dinner of crispy fried duck. As the band had begun to take off in America, in no time we were sent back into the studio to make another record. Like the previous two, we recorded *No Heavy Petting* with Leo Lyons once more, but added a new band member. Michael's guitar parts had got to be quite intricate. He would have been able to layer them in the studio, but that would have meant that a whole level dropped out of our sound whenever we played the new songs live. Our solution was to bring in a keyboard player to enhance us on record and on stage. Danny Peyronel had spent a couple of years playing with the Heavy Metal Kids and was a good musician, but our experiment with him didn't really work out. Whereas Paul Chapman had filled us out, Danny softened us and his spell in the band proved to be very short-lived.

There were some strong songs on *No Heavy Petting*, like 'Natural Thing' and 'I'm a Loser', but it wasn't as well received as *Force It*. In America, it barely crept into the Top 200 but that was more down to the situation at the record company. Up until then, Chrysalis's records had been distributed by Warner Brothers in the States, which was a major operation. However, they had decided to go independent and that hurt our album in particular since we were almost a test case. In effect, Chrysalis failed to get the record into the chart-return stores. At the time, Gary Wright had a hit album in the States with *Dream Weaver*. We found out later that *No Heavy Petting* was selling as many copies as his record, but most of our sales didn't get logged.

It would be another three years before the songs on *Phenomenon*, *Force It* and *No Heavy Petting* really made their mark. None of those records got better than lukewarm reviews when they were first released. It used to drive me round the bend. Geoff Barton, the chief rock critic at *Sounds*, for example, would basically write that our albums were all right, but not as fantastic as Kiss's. Then I'd bump into Geoff a month or so later, and he'd tell me our record had really grown on him. I used to wonder why he couldn't have listened to it more before he reviewed it.

In a flash, we were back to being a four-piece again, with Michael having to work harder. Fortunately, we went out on the road in America and were able to put our troubles behind us. We did our first Day on the Green show to 55,000 people in San Francisco, which really showed us we were getting through to American audiences, and then went out as the middle band of a three-group bill with Nazareth as headliners and Savoy Brown. That tour marked our card to Paul Raymond, who played keyboards and rhythm guitar for Savoy Brown, and we wasted no time in recruiting him once we'd completed the dates.

Bringing Paul into the band allowed us to create the quintessential UFO sound, which was made up of two guitars *and* keyboards. In that sense, Paul was our definitive musician. He was a nice enough guy, too, and like us had a great sense of fun, but Paul was also even older than Phil and could be a bit of a cynic. The best word for him, I think, would be outspoken. For no apparent reason, he would quite often say things that could be demeaning or hurtful to other people. However, Paul was a vital part of the band and he and Andy soon enough formed a bond – a sort of breakaway rebellion. That allowed them to ignore the twaddle that Phil and I often talked and put us in good shape to make our next, all-important album at the start of 1977.

After the relative failure of *No Heavy Petting*, Phil insisted that we needed a new producer and, from someone at Chrysalis, got hold of Ron Nevison's phone number. Ron had worked with Led Zeppelin on *Physical Graffiti*, the Who on *Quadrophenia*, and recorded the first couple of Bad Company albums, which I had loved. He had got a great sound on all of those records too, so getting him would be a real coup for us. Phil called Ron and managed to convince him to fly over to London from LA and produce *Lights Out*.

It quickly became apparent to us that Ron was like no one else we had worked with to that point. Physically, he wasn't a particularly imposing guy, but he was domineering and would shout and bark orders at the band, the engineers and anyone who had the misfortune to cross his path. If you turned up at the studio and hadn't learned your parts for the day, he would go ballistic, his face turning red and steam almost coming out of his ears. At first, we determined that he was like a schoolmaster, and even bought him a cane, black gown and mortarboard. But as Ron's eruptions grew more volcanic, we decided that 'despot' was a better description for him and on the finished album he was credited as 'Ronnie Fury'. Ron liked to live the high life, too. If we went out to a restaurant, he would say to us, 'Watch this, guys, it'll blow her socks off', and then hand the waitress a hundred pounds tip. He also told us that he had two Rolls-Royce cars with number plates that read 'Greed' and 'Envy', which pretty much summed him up. After a day's work, Ron liked to kick back and hold court. There was never a lot of warmth in his voice when he talked about Zeppelin, though. He used to tell us stories about making *Physical Graffiti* with them at Headley Grange in Hampshire and how they would smash up the antiques all around the old house. It wasn't actually their acts of vandalism that aggrieved Ron, but the fact that he had been billed, in part, for the damage.

In total, we spent a couple of months butting heads with Ron at Air Studios on Oxford Street, but though his methods were unorthodox, they worked for us. Each day's session would start at noon and to begin with Ron complained about a lack of energy in the room. But quite quickly he established that there were two reasons for our indolence. One, the booze hadn't arrived. Two, there was no cocaine. Thereafter, Ron would ensure to have drinks set up when we arrived and then run around to each member of the band with a small silver spoon and a hit of cocaine. As if by magic, we would be able to cut a basic track in five minutes and one take. So, thanks to Ron, I discovered the importance of getting yourself in the right mood to make music.

A further initiative of Ron's was to bring in a string arrangement for the album's big ballad, 'Love to Love'. Phil and I turned up one afternoon and there was a string section and conductor in the studio. Bear in mind we just got to hear them overdub the song, and out of context, but I told Ron it sounded fucking awful, like Des O'Connor. Ron, though, had such great ears he could have heard a pin drop and he was proved right. When I heard the finished track, my jaw hit the floor; it sounded so stirring, so vast, and was an instant classic. *Lights Out* as a whole was a huge turning point for us. Once it came out, people started to take us more seriously, and especially in the States. In a way, though, America was there for the taking. By that time, Zeppelin would only tour every two or three years and Sabbath had just put out their least good album to that point, *Technical Ecstasy*, and were on the wane. We, on the other hand, were peaking and right in people's faces. We'd also got great songs *and* Michael Schenker. Michael could conjure an idea out of nowhere. You would have something that you knew could be a good song, like 'Too Hot to Handle' or 'Lights Out' itself, but for the fact it was perhaps just too short or repetitive, and suddenly Michael would come up with a bridge or new section that would take it to a whole other level.

Nevertheless, it never was plain sailing for us. To launch the album, we were booked onto an American arena tour with Rush, and on the eve of it starting, Michael went missing. He gave us no warning or explanation as to why he cleared off, and no idea of where he'd gone, but by then I didn't expect him to. Increasingly, Michael was temperamental and the littlest thing could bring him to the boil: being booked into the wrong sort of hotel, a poor show, or being taken to a bad bar.

I had the utmost respect for him as a musician, but didn't always understand him as a person. In this instance, our attitude was to view Michael's vanishing act as nothing more than a hiccup, like, 'Oh well, he's gone', and it wouldn't be for the last time. I mean to say, Michael even ended up walking out on the Michael Schenker Group. We brought Paul Chapman back to stand in for him on the first leg of shows with Rush and they went well. Oddly enough, no sooner had *Lights Out* become a US Top 30 album than Michael decided to come back. He has always insisted that this fact didn't influence him in the slightest, and I have to take him at his word. I actually went over to London to fetch him and flew back with him and his girlfriend to the States.

Michael Schenker: I really didn't like success or fame. In fact, I ran away when I found out that Lights Out *was in the American charts. I didn't want the pressure of having to do this or that, or to be here and there. And it was Pete who talked me back into the band.*

We hit it off with Rush more or less straight away, which was a first for us. They didn't mind if we made jokes about their music or stage gear, or our extra-curricular activities. But then, at the time the three of them *were* playing these elaborate prog-rock epics and did step out on stage in Japanese kimonos. In particular, Geddy Lee, their bassist and singer, and guitarist Alex Lifeson were a joy to be around. For years afterwards, I would go round to Geddy's house whenever we were in Toronto. I would have our tour bus park at the end of his road and used to move all the bloody awful Yes albums from the front to the back of his record collection. Geddy once told me that I fell off the stage mid–song during one show on that tour. I don't recall doing so, but it's entirely possible. There were also plenty of unintended theatrics that went on during the Rush show. They would use so much dry ice that Phil and I were able to crawl around onstage unseen while they were playing. Michael and I would also on occasion finish their set off for them. Their road crew would hand us their guitars and the two of us would bash out the last crescendo of notes from the side of the stage, while Geddy and Alex buggered off back to their dressing room.

Geddy Lee, Rush: You know, to be frank, I don't remember Pete ever coming to visit me at my home in Toronto. I do, though, remember him falling off stage on two occasions on that tour. The second time, the three of us in Rush were sat talking in our dressing room and Pete's bass just vanished from the stage. It was like, 'Uh-oh, Pete's gone over the edge again'. But everybody partied back then; we were all of us younger and making the most of our opportunity to be out on the road.

That tour was my introduction to UFO and their music. They were all very friendly, but you couldn't help but notice that they would all be in their cups, shall we say, and before every show. They would pound a few drinks and then hit the stage flying. That was their thing. I recall us doing one show in a dry county in Texas, which meant there was no alcohol allowed in the building. We were backstage and I'd heard that the UFO guys were really bitching and moaning about not having any booze. I looked out of our dressing-room window into the car park, and there they all were in their stage gear, brown-bagging it out the boot of their car. Hey, necessity is the mother of adventure.

They were also always insulting each other for the sake of humour. That soon extended to us, which I took to be a good sign and a compliment. We used to play the song Xanadu at the time, and yes, all kinds of dry ice would come on stage. Pete and Phil Mogg would stand at the side of the stage and yell things about honeydew and melons at us, because one of the lines in the song goes, 'I have dined on honeydew'. On one occasion, they even snuck up on stage and nailed a pair of slippers beside my foot pedals. There the slippers were when the dry ice dissipated, I guess to go along with my kimono.

Pete and I spent a lot of time together on the tour and I enjoyed his company a lot. He was, of course, a very different kind of musician to me. He was this guy in skin-tight pants with his shag haircut and playing his big Thunderbird bass. He had a typical Thunderbird sound, too, with a really heavy bottom end. He described it to me once as, 'Three-quarters nice, one-quarter not very nice.'

Whenever Pete's name comes up between the three of us today, we all smile. He was a lot of fun to be around, but also very sweet. He truly was a wouldn't-hurt-a-fly kind of guy and dedicated to his music. And he was very rock and roll. I was on our tour bus one time and listening to the new Bill Bruford solo album, which had just then come out. There was a great bass player on that record named Jeff Berlin, and it was pretty complex sort of jazz-rock. Pete came stumbling aboard the bus and was just appalled by the sound of it. He sat down beside me and said, as if in profound pain, 'Glee,', which he used to call me, 'don't listen to this, it isn't rock and roll.' You know, Pete's a rocker at heart and he's remained true to that from the music that he's played to the way that he's lived his life.

———

After the Rush tour we also went out with Kiss, but our record had begun to sell and it soon reached the point where we were able to do our own shows at some of the big places we had played with those bands. That was the way it worked in America. It was a slog, but certain cities would eventually take to you and then a promoter in one of them would risk putting you on as a main attraction. It felt as though America had opened up to us. More and more people were coming to our shows, and you can't play to audiences of sixteen to seventeen thousand a night and fail to think you've broken big. In the next couple of years I would read about all these British punk and new wave bands in *Sounds* or the *NME*, and they would claim to be big in America. No, they weren't. The truth is that those bands only did club shows, whereas we were filling up sports arenas. And we'd got there the hard way by touring non-stop all over the country, playing with established acts and learning from them. It was also a fact that we thought we were better than any other band. By that point, I could even find fault with Zeppelin and firmly believed we would be able to play with anyone and steal the show.

We spent so much time out in the States, three or four months at a stretch, that Wilf decided that the band should relocate to LA. It made sense to have a base that we could fly in and out of more easily, but the pity of it was that Jo and I had just then been offered the chance to buy the flat we had been renting in St John's Wood, and for next to nothing. The managing agent only wanted something like £30,000 for it, which was a steal, but we went off to California instead. I could kick myself now, because today that place would be worth an absolute fortune. But then, I suppose in many ways that's the story of my life.

In LA, we happened across a brand-new, very modern-looking apartment block in Studio City, which couldn't have been more different from where we'd left. Phil and Paul Raymond both had young families by then, so they got themselves houses just five minutes up the road from Jo and me, as did Michael. Andy was a bit further out in Ventura. Typically, though, it was me who was lucky enough to end up living as neighbour to one of the biggest drug dealers in the city.

Over the road from our block, there was a gay bar and its customers would often park their cars across our driveway. One night, this guy (let's call him Rick) and I both ran down to the street at the same time to move someone along. The two of us struck up a conversation and Rick asked me what I did for a living, and then invited me up to his apartment to check out his line of business. Bloody hell, I couldn't believe my eyes. In his place, Rick had literally sack-loads of cocaine. In the front room, there was a pile of coke tipped out on a mirror. It was a small, perfectly formed mountain of brilliant-white, and I leapt upon it.

Soon enough, I became Rick's best friend and most reliable customer. His apartment was modest, nondescript, which allowed him to keep a low profile, and he had a front of a clothing business that didn't actually exist. He was very careful with the doorbell, that's for sure, but must have been making an absolute fortune. Rick sold coke to Marlon Brandon, a who's who of other 'A' list Hollywood stars and most of the top music executives in the city. And in all the years that we lived in LA, I never went without a line. Many was the time I left Rick's place totally wired and would then lie in our bed, wide awake and watch the clock tick round until it was time to leave for the airport.

A few years later, after Jo and I had moved back to London, I happened to be in LA for my birthday. I was staying at the

Sunset Marquis hotel and when I got back to my room that night, Rick had beaten me to it. He'd taken a big mirror off the wall and written out on it the words 'Happy Birthday Pete' in fat lines of prime-quality cocaine. The two of us did an ounce together, Rick drove home at four in the morning and then I did a second ounce on my own. I'd have to say that Rick was a very bad influence on me.

There were also more practical advantages to living in LA. Wherever the band was on tour in the US, if we had a day off I was able to take a night flight and spend it at home. I used especially to enjoy coming in from the cold of the East Coast and arriving in LA with the sun up. The next day, I'd return to the tour feeling rejuvenated, which was important to me, because our schedule was relentless. In fact, I can't recall Jo and me ever being able to go on holiday together, or even a time when I could just sit out in the garden for a couple of days. I got so used to the layout of hotel rooms that when I was at home, I would find myself in the middle of the night going for a pee in the wardrobe.

Jo embraced the LA lifestyle, too. We'd dine out every night when I was at home and she could shop for clothes on Melrose Avenue. And I saw the rest of the guys in the band on and off whenever we were all in town. We would meet up at the Rainbow Bar & Grill, and, to be honest, on such occasions the drink-driving rules would go right out of the window. At first, I rented a Camaro and then I got hold of a Corvette, but I tended to be a little erratic behind the wheel of a high-performance sports car. Phil had a Trans Am. Andy, of course, got himself a Toyota Celica because he said he got much better mileage to the gallon – in the country with the cheapest petrol in the world.

Quite often, Phil and I would race each other home in our cars. To get to Studio City from the Rainbow we had to cross Laurel Canyon and the roads were narrow and winding. It was like a test of skill and daring to take them at high speed and things were liable to get a little careless, because I at least would push sobriety to the max and our races grew increasingly more hair-raising. One evening, I got pulled up for speeding right in front of our apartment. The cop actually asked me what the new Camaro was like. I told him: 'Fast.'

Another time, we had a Cadillac on rent for the whole band. Phil was our designated driver and his speciality was to collide with a selection of other cars and then keep going. On this particular occasion, Phil bashed the Cadillac into a car on one side of the street, then a car on the other, and then drove off as fast as he could to escape the crowd of people brought out by the terrible noise. Somehow or other, I never had a major car accident in LA. I had people go into the back of me, but would shrug it off because I had a stash of drugs in the car.

Otherwise, being at home was more of a return to reality, which didn't do me any harm, and at such times I led quite a normal, domesticated life. I'd shop for food, that kind of thing. I'd also go round to Paul Raymond's quite a bit. The two of us would spend the day playing loud music and drink a bottle of Jack Daniel's, or else I'd do a few lines. Such short interludes aside, though, it was left to Jo to make sure everything was taken care of in our ordinary life, while I went off and raised hell. In that sense, ours was very much a Jekyll and Hyde kind of relationship.

I would call Jo from the road as often as I could, but it wasn't as easy to keep in touch in those days as it is now. And the other-women situation had extended to the point where a senator's wife turned up backstage at one of our shows and wanted to party with me. I wasn't sure what her husband's politics were, but she definitely enjoyed Jack Daniel's and nose candy and the two of us had a very nice time together, thank you very much. The more success we were having, though, the more girls there were willing to do the most outrageous things. I became almost desensitized and eventually no longer wanted to have sex with every single one of them. It was as if there was nothing left that could shock or surprise me and every day was like living in a nuthouse.

CHAPTER 6

A young man's further travels through the American heartland
being attended to by women of dubious morals
and surrendering to illicit temptation.

———

Joe Elliott: *UFO had a huge impact on Def Leppard. When we first got together, we spent months pretty much just rehearsing, and that summer of 1977, we took a band holiday on a boat on the Norfolk Broads. UFO were on their* Lights Out *tour, and it turned out they were doing a gig at the Ipswich Gaumont, which was near enough down the road from us. The five of us went along – that was in the days when you could turn up and pay on the door. Our guitarist, Steve Clark, was so knocked out by seeing that gig, and Michael Schenker in particular, that he threatened to quit our band if we didn't start doing our own shows. That was just the kick up the arse that we needed.*

Ross Halfin: *I was the exception to the rule, because with UFO I thought it was the bassist and singer that were really good rather than the guitarist. Pete and Phil were great together at that point. There* *was a sort of gang-like quality to them and they were a dastardly duo. Pete in particular had also found his look by then, with his Thunderbird bass and his LA-style outfits. And he looked great, like the perfect, quintessential rock star.*

There was only one other guy I saw who ever played the bass like me. His name was John Wood but everyone knew him as Junior, and he used to play in one of Steve Howe's (of Yes fame) earliest bands, Tomorrow. This was during London's psychedelic era in the late-1960s and, like me, Junior would move around on stage a lot. I saw Tomorrow quite a few times at one club or other and he made a definite impression on me.

It was an unwritten rule that the bass player was supposed to stand rooted to the spot, but people have often told me that I was more like a frontman on stage. At any rate, I was never still. Not that I had a choice but to step forward in UFO. Phil would stand back on stage quite a bit and Michael was soloing, so someone needed to gee up the audience. Truthfully, I also think I did all that running and leaping about in order to hide my inabilities, though it was actually quite tricky to be so active and have to play. I had to make sure that my fingers were in the right place on the frets, particularly if I'd raced from one side of the stage to the other, dropped to my knees and then lay spread-eagled on the stage. The spotlight might not have followed me and I'd be in blackout, trying to feel my way in the dark. In fact, I got quite accomplished at navigating my way blind along the neck of the bass or at least at covering up my mistakes.

And yes, I liked to have flash clothes, too. As a band, we tried quite hard to put over a certain kind of glamorous look but without being glam-rock. I suppose that had something

From left: brother Neil, mum Ruth, the author and dad Fred: 'They were good, kind parents but they didn't suffer fools.' *(Author's Collection)*

A family holiday in Braine-l'Alleud, Belgium, 1962. From left: the author, great uncle Paulin, Neil, Ruth, Joelle, great aunt Elisabeth, Denis and Martine. *(Author's Collection)*

(above and right) 'Bloody hell, for a young lad it was truly unbelievable what went on.' *(Nikma/Dalle/IconicPix)*

(below) Ready for lift-off. UFO in 1973 – from left: the author, Andy Parker, Phil Mogg and new recruit, German guitar wunderkind Michael Schenker: '[With Michael] there were no rules and it was so much more exciting.' *(© GAB Archive/Getty Images)*

UFO onstage at the Marquee Club circa 1974. Said Schenker: 'Pete was never what you would call technical on bass, but all heart.' *(MM-Media Archive/IconicPix)*

In the US on 1975's *Force It* tour: 'It was our going off to America that hastened the end of my first marriage.' *(© Jorgen Angel/Getty Images)*

UFO circa 1976's *No Heavy Pettin* album. From left – the short-lived Danny Peyronel, Parker, Mogg, the author and Schenker. *(© Jorgen Angel/Getty Images)*

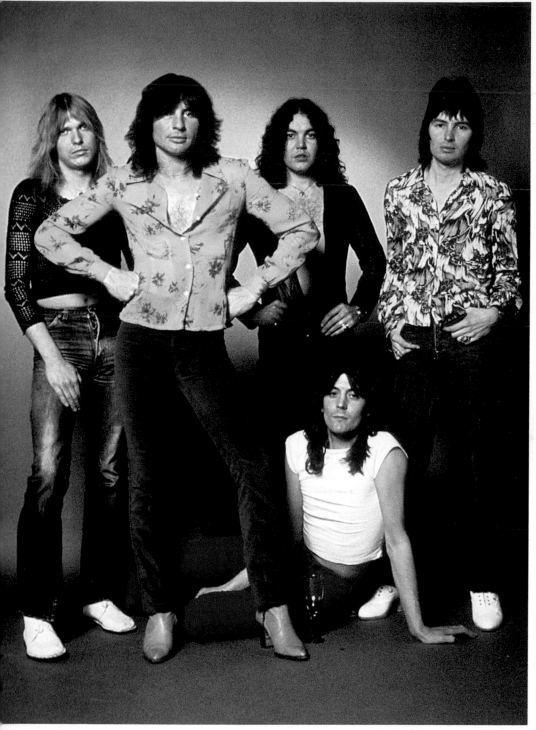

The classic line-up, 1977: from left – Schenker, Mogg, Parker, the author and Paul Raymond.
© *GAB Archive/Getty Images*

The author in classic late-70s live pose. Says Geddy Lee of Rush: 'Pete had a typical Thunderbird bass sound. He described it to me once as, "Three quarters nice, one quarter not so nice."'
(© Tony Mottram)

1978's classic *Obsession* album hits the US and the UK via a Sunset Strip billboard and mock-press campaign: 'That was the only question Michael ever asked about our artwork: why he didn't also get to have balls on his eyes.' *(© Pictorial Press Ltd/Alamy Stock Photo)*

From 1979's US tour with AC/DC to promote *Strangers in the Night*: 'I pulled out a stash of coke and Angus Young peered over at me and said: "Here, Pete, you want to get yourself a good breakfast instead of that stuff."'

Backstage at Hammersmith Odeon with AC/DC's Bon Scott, 7 February 1980. Twelve days later, Scott was dead. *(© Ross Halfin)*

to do with us all having been teenage Mods. We used to shop at a boutique called Biba's in Kensington Market. It was pretty much exclusively women's clothes that we bought, but I don't think we wore them in an effeminate way. Years later, it was quite flattering for me to see Steve Harris of Iron Maiden and then Nikki Sixx in Mötley Crüe wearing exactly the kind of zebra-striped trousers that I'd had in UFO. Steve in particular made no bones about taking his look from me, but good luck to both of them. They're certainly richer men than me these days.

On stage, we took things very seriously in UFO, almost too much so. In the end, to avoid petty or more physical disputes, we made a pact between the five of us not to talk about a gig immediately afterwards. What could be a casual remark about somebody making a mistake in a certain song was liable to turn into a full-blown argument. It was Michael who was most likely to make that kind of comment, especially to me. If he was doing a solo, Michael would get particularly irate if he thought I was being too theatrical, and I guess taking the attention away from him. On a couple of occasions, I was running around like a madman and kicked his leads out, or else trod on his pedals. He was quite relaxed about it the first time: 'Oh, this happens, Pete.' The second time, though, he was fucking furious and actually threatened to kill me.

I used to play very loud, too, so Phil would always be fighting a lost cause to be heard over me and Michael as well. During a gig, Phil would regularly sidle up to my amps and turn them down. Of course, I'd then turn them up again. At one show in the States, Phil got so upset with this state of affairs that he stormed off to side stage, took a fireman's axe off a wall, and then stomped back on and put it through one of the monitors. God knows what the audience thought.

No sooner had *Lights Out* begun selling well in America than we tore up our tour budget. Instead of minding the pennies, it became more of a case of do what you like. There was just more of everything. The backstage rider was as resplendent as the menu in a fine-dining restaurant. Just like the sex, the booze and drugs were also on tap. I never actually felt drunk or hungover, but that was probably because of all the coke I was doing. You tend not to get headaches when you're hoovering up South America's finest.

And we were all at it. Later on, Michael claimed that it was the rest of us in the band who had encouraged him to start drinking heavily. However, I don't remember that he ever required too much help in that regard, and we all suffered the consequences. There was one time we were in Kentucky and Michael went on the rampage. First off, he did a considerable amount of rearranging to his hotel room and then, at a certain point in the afternoon, he was spied up on the roof of the building, attempting to wrench out the electric cabling with his bare hands. The hotel manager, of course, called the police. Soon enough, Michael was ordered down and our tour manager rushed to the front desk to try and smooth things over. Just as he was pleading that we had to leave for the venue, the attending cop made a comment to Michael, who replied, and I quote, 'Fuck off, you cunt.' At which point, Michael also pulled out a water pistol and doused the cop and the hotel manager. Michael was duly hauled off downtown, and our by-now-frantic tour manager followed with the money to bail him out. He arrived at the station house to discover that Michael had pulled the sink off the wall in his holding cell and flooded the place. That was the end of that gig.

I don't believe I ever wrecked a hotel room myself. But then, you don't when you've got drugs in the room. Hotel security guards were generally off-duty cops, so the last thing I'd want would be to alert them to anything untoward. For the same reason, I kept my music reasonably quiet. Anything so there wouldn't be a knock on the door in the middle of the night when I'd got half an ounce of coke on the bedside table. Fans would also sleep on the floor outside of our rooms. That started to get a bit daunting – stepping out of the room and having people literally lying in wait for you. After several months of that, there was nothing I craved more than a bit of peace and quiet.

By the end of the *Lights Out* tour, I had also started to use heroin. As I said, I'd tried it when I was thirteen, but I took to it much slower than to cocaine. It was reintroduced to me by a dealer – but it could as well have been by anybody around us at that time – to be used as part of a speedball with cocaine. To be honest, by then I would try anything that was put in front of me. But the way it was explained, it made perfect sense to me to take heroin like that. Coke allowed me to talk all night and appear interesting, but the trouble was that I would be wired for hours at a time. The heroin in a speedball took the edge off the cocaine high and allowed me to come down.

To begin with, it was more of a recreational thing after a show, and I wasn't injecting it at that point but would snort it. Prior to then, my recipe for a good show was to have a nap in the afternoon, go down to the venue for our sound-check, play the gig and then break out the cocaine. I'd then have to take a handful of sleeping pills to knock me out. The speedballs

89

had the same sort of effect as the pills, but more pleasant, so the way I looked at it was that I had increased my options. Funnily enough, I was with Michael one night, doing coke, and I also did a line of heroin. He looked accusingly at me and said, 'If you make the mistake of giving this to me and it kills me, I will make sure to murder you first.'

Michael Schenker: In general, Pete had style and rock-and-roll attitude. He told little white lies all the time, made things up about this and that and would borrow things from other people, mainly money, which no one ever got back. But that didn't matter to me, because he struck me as a pure, innocent character. Personally, I think people took advantage of him a lot. He was a man without boundaries, which was very dangerous. I could understand that, because the two of us came from a similar place in that respect. I think my whole life has been about me trying to understand where the borderlines are found. Pete couldn't see those and many times he crossed over the line, or let other people take him over it. He is an extreme person, which is why his downfall was so dramatic.

———

We made our next album, *Obsession*, in LA, once again with the inimitable Ron Nevison. The basic tracks were done at a place on Western Avenue in an area of the city that's now called Korea Town. It was an old studio from the 1940s, but had been gutted, so it was an empty, cavernous space, perfect for the big sound we were going after. For the overdubs, Ron moved us to a disused post office in Beverley Hills, the 3rd Street Postal Carrying Station. He rented the Record Plant mobile and rolled that up outside in the car park.

First day at the post office, we turned up to find the building had been filled with an assortment of even more decrepit sofas and chairs. Ron had been up the road to a second-hand store, a Mexican place, and rented a job lot of furniture to give the place some atmosphere, or so he claimed. If you so much as brushed against anything, clouds of dust would rise up into the air. It was bloody awful and Phil flat out refused to sit down, so that was a good start. Next day, Ron had got rid of all of his bargains and forked out for a decent couch.

We had other small victories over him, too. Ron set us up in the warehouse and rigged up a camera and speaker so he could see and talk to us from his vantage point in the mobile truck. It wasn't long before I moved the speaker into the restroom. From then on, whenever he barked out his orders it sounded as if he was sitting on the loo. Mike Clink, who was Ron's understudy and engineer, found that extremely funny, but he had to be careful. Mike was not allowed to laugh at Ron, or even to sit in his designated chair. It stood Mike in good stead, because later on he would have to manage Axl Rose when he produced Guns N' Roses' *Appetite for Destruction* album.

Mike Clink, engineer on **Obsession:** *Ron Nevison was a no-nonsense kind of guy who didn't have a whole lot of patience for anybody. That was just his particular MO. But Pete and Phil Mogg pretty much constantly looked for ways to wind Ron up; they were partners in crime and played off each other. Of course, as well as Ron's speaker, they constantly moved his camera so he couldn't see what was going on, and that drove him more mad than anything.*

Even more so than Ron, though, Michael Schenker was not the kind of guy to put up with Pete and Phil's shenanigans. I certainly never saw him get involved in any of the supposed fun that those guys had. In fact, there was very little conversation between them in the studio that I noted. Michael was pretty much of a loner. He would come in each day, sit in the studio lounge on his own, practise his guitar, drink a beer and eat mash potato. And that was just about all that he did during our whole time together on that record.

Certainly, when Pete was able to have a couple of drinks in the studio then he relaxed a bit. But just about everybody I've worked with thinks that they play better when they've imbibed. A lot of musicians I've dealt with have had dependency problems with alcohol or drugs, and the thing is when you do that every day of your life, it becomes your reality. To be straight is not to be normal, but I never saw Pete be totally out of it in the studio. Actually, I always thought of Pete as a very capable musician. By that I mean, his choice of notes and general performance was good. I don't recall having to spend an exorbitant amount of time with him doing overdubs. He came in, was well rehearsed and knew his parts. In fact, part of the problem was that he accomplished them relatively quickly. Once he was done with his work and had idle time on his hands, Pete would be constantly on the lookout for something to occupy him. And definitely, then he would let loose.

Every day with Ron was a different story, but he had his odd routines. We got used to Mike telling us that Ron had just slipped out for an hour; we never found out to where but he was always perked up when he returned. He also brought any number of girls down to the studio with him. There was one girl in particular, a dark-haired Canadian, who came by a couple of times and struck us as being extremely stuck-up, which never went down well with the band. Ron liked to show her off, though. And her pride and joy was her sports car, an open-top Austin-Healey. The second time she came to see Ron, Phil and I went out into the car park, let the handbrake off the Austin-Healey and pushed it around to the other side of the building. We expended more bloody energy on that car than we did on our own record. When Ron's special friend came back out and thought someone had nicked her prized car, she lost her mind. Ron went ballistic too, but he knew exactly who was behind it. In fact, he went on strike until the two of us pushed it back. Four years later, I saw a photo of the very same girl in an American newspaper. Her name was Cathy Smith and she'd been with the comedian John Belushi on the night he died at the Chateau Marmont Hotel. It was Cathy who apparently injected Belushi with the speedball that killed him and she ended up serving fifteen months in jail. Next to that, I don't suppose losing her car for an afternoon would have seemed such a big deal.

Another mistake Ron made was to invite his mum along to the studio. This little old lady turned up one afternoon, though she was probably the same age then that I am now. While Ron sat at the mixing desk being super-critical of what we'd recorded that day, Phil and I grilled his mum about what he was like as a child. She told us all sorts of stuff, but the thing I remember most was that she called him 'little Ronnie'. After a while, Ron suddenly exploded. He fumed at her, 'For fuck's sake, Ma, don't tell these assholes any more', and then frog-marched her out of the studio. And that was the last we saw of Mrs Nevison.

Despite all that, one night Ron did actually invite us up to his house in Bel-Air for dinner. He'd gone out and bought all this gourmet food especially for the occasion, but somehow or other we forgot to turn up. Next day, Ron was absolutely seething, but not so much at us. It turned out his cat had snuck into the fridge and eaten Ron's selection of fine meats. He told us he'd put his boot up the poor animal's arse, which of course was music to our ears.

Yet another thing which sent Ron's blood pressure boiling was the endless amount of time Phil would spend on his lyrics. To be fair, you'd think Phil was writing *War and Peace*. Ron would scream at Phil, punch the studio walls, but in the end even he would have to beg Phil, to get him to finish. Given how much attention most people paid to the words, Phil might just as well have scribbled 'Hickory Dickory Dock . . .' and saved all of us the grief. However, we did also get some work done. In fact, to many fans of the band, *Obsession* is our definitive studio album and it certainly captured that line-up of the band at its peak. In our own way we were all songwriters, especially Phil, Michael and me, and we'd played together so much by then it was like second nature. A lot of the songs on that album were written in their rough form in a half-hour or so, as if God-given. The music just seemed to flow out of us. I used to write a lot at home, and an idea for a song could just as easily pop into my head over breakfast or at three in the morning. I got into the habit of putting everything straight down on a little portable tape machine so nothing got lost.

It's difficult for me now to pick out the songs I'm most proud of. The opening track, 'Only You Can Rock Me', would be one. I'd got the basic idea for it, a driving rocker, and being the genius that he is, Michael came up with the section halfway through – that sort of dreamy-sounding bridge and then his soaring solo – which switched it up from being a classic rock thing into a completely different gear. 'Cherry' is another special song for me and has a great bass line. It's more like a lead guitar part. I used to practise doing high notes, which is why I was able to come up with so many melodies. I haven't heard too many other bassists do the kind of thing that I did on that song, and certainly not in hard rock. At other times, I'd stick to basics because there'd be nothing worse for Michael than me competing with him when he was doing a guitar solo. In general, though, it was the fact that each of us was able to contribute to the songs that gave us such a strong sense of camaraderie.

Joe Elliott: It was only later on that I found out that a lot of those classic songs were written by Pete, like 'Too Hot to Handle', 'Out in the Street' and 'Only You Can Rock Me'. Often as not with great rock and roll, it's more about the attitude than the musicianship, and that's pretty obviously the case with Pete. You could teach a gorilla to play 'Too Hot to Handle', but it's such a memorable song to my generation of rock fans. But then all of the UFO stuff from that era is pivotal and totally timeless.

The action on one of Pete's basses was so off I'm sure you could have slept under the strings – they must have been an inch off the neck, but he didn't want to be Jaco Pastorius. Pete's a one-fingered bassist, a notch or two up from Sid Vicious, but he looked the part and went bonkers on stage. He was the perfect visual balance to Schenker's sheer awesomeness and his presence was so much more important to that band than what he was playing.

Ross Halfin: Every album that UFO made with Schenker is good, but Lights Out *and* Obsession *in particular were great. That line-up of the band was outstanding. In fact, if I had to name my top ten bands of all time, that version of UFO would be one of them, right up there alongside the Who, Zeppelin and the Stones. They were all great players, a brilliant live band and hugely influential on countless bands that came along after them. At their peak they couldn't be touched, really they couldn't.*

———

I knew we'd made it when *Obsession* came out. I'd be driving my Corvette down Sunset Strip at eleven in the morning, put on the local rock radio station and 'Only You Can Rock Me' would come on. And that happened every day. There was also a giant billboard of the album cover posted up on the Strip, so it felt to me as if we'd taken over the place, like the new kings.

That was the last-but-one of those great album covers that Hipgnosis did for us. Phil, Michael and I were photographed for the front cover. The shoot was done at a veterinary clinic at UCLA. Phil and I were stood in the foreground with our hair slicked back, and afterwards they superimposed all these metal ball-bearings onto our faces. I have no idea why that was, but I was always very happy to go along with Hipgnosis's ideas. By contrast, Michael was left unblemished and looked like a Greek god. Still today, that is the only question he has ever asked about our artwork: why he didn't also get to have balls on his eyes.

The American tour for *Obsession* was like a victory lap for us. The album had gone into the *Billboard* chart with a bullet and almost every show we did was an arena gig. On the first leg we went out with Blue Oyster Cult. They were good guys and had not long had a massive hit with '(Don't Fear) The Reaper', but they weren't able to follow us on stage. We'd finish our set and half the audience would walk out. People were coming along to the shows just to see us.

One of the best things about that tour, though, was how we travelled. Prior to then, a significant portion of each day would be spent sat around the hotel, and that would be when I'd get most restless. I'd even started to bend my rule and do a little toot of coke during the daytime as well as after the show. Fortunately, the success of the album convinced Wilf to get us our own tour bus. It was one of those big, sleek, silver machines that you see in the movies and became a real sanctuary for me. As we drove through the night from town to town, drink and drugs were always freely available and sleep wasn't a priority for me. If I was up till six in the morning, I'd simply stay on the bus and not bother going to bed in the hotel. On more than one occasion, I was up for two, three or even four days straight, but in general I needed a day off after a night's debauchery because by then I'd put pretty much everything that was on offer into my system. Having the bus also meant I didn't have to start each day with a couple of large Bloody Marys just to be able to cope with getting on a plane.

Silly things would otherwise keep our spirits up. At one point we bought a crockpot and would make stews on the bus instead of having to pull over to eat. It was ridiculous really. I would be doing a line of coke, the whole point of which was to suppress your appetite, and at the same time concocting a gourmet feast in the sort of pot my mum would have used. Sadly, our tour manager threw the crockpot off the bus in the end, because a certain band member objected to the smell of the cooking. That and the fact we had started to have armies of rats congregating under the bus whenever we parked up. Aside from the band and crew, the only other people permitted on the bus were drug dealers and hand-picked women. We had developed a well-practised selection policy for girls and had the crew filter them for us. Except that it would cause problems when one of the crew thought he had picked up the most glamorous girl in the venue and all of a sudden she would be whisked off by a member of the band. Truly, because of all the trouble that it led to, one of the regrets I have now is that there were too many women about. It reached the point where I'd always have to make excuses: not letting one girl up to my hotel room because I already had another up there on the go, not to mention keeping Jo off the case. Today, I do feel guilty about how I behaved to the women in my life, of course I do. But then, I was like a kid let loose in a candy store. I mean, I'd never imagined that so many girls would seem so fanatical about my body. No doubt about it, it was great for the first two or three years that we toured America. But by the time of *Obsession*, the girls had begun to fly into our shows from all over the country and it did my head in trying to keep track of who was coming and going. The whole thing just got to be exhausting. Years later, I found out that Mötley Crüe had a very effective way of getting rid of unwanted women. Once they had done the dirty deed, they would get their tour manager to call each of their rooms, claim they were being summoned to a band meeting and then exit en masse. For my part, I would just say I was popping to so-and-so's room, and then not come back. It was the same story for the girls. You'd sleep with a girl and next thing she'd be telling you how she'd fucked David Lee Roth the week before and that he was just the best.

Girls were something else that Michael was funny about. There was a time we were in Munich and Phil and I climbed over his hotel balcony just to get a look into his room. There was Michael, laid on his back in bed with a girl straddling and riding him. He was, though, smoking and had headphones on. He told me the next day that he had been listening to a recording of that night's gig. Michael would listen back to every show we did just to pick out the mistakes, and I think he thought the girls should do all of the other work.

The hangers-on – who were convenient because you could rely on them for a couple of lines of coke – also became boring. It was not as if we had anything else to talk to them about. By then, we were doing huge venues like the Forum in LA. We had to have our own meet-and-greet areas set up backstage, because it wasn't possible to fit fifty groupies and drug dealers into a single dressing room. Once again, that was good fun for the first week of a tour, but you can't keep up that sort of pace permanently, so you start to slow down. To escape, I liked to go off with a member of the crew and find a quiet bar or pub. Even then, a lot of drinking went on and invariably I'd get into trouble. More than once I had a bar manager bang on a toilet door, because I'd been in there for an unfathomably long time. And then I'd reel out with coke smeared all over my face.

For all that, my memories of the period are for the most part fond. We'd had nothing but success since moving to LA. We had decent places to live, nice cars, travelled first class, stayed in good hotels, and there were more and more people who loved the band. It was rare, too, that we ever played a bad show – there was a level of performance that we were determined to maintain. The more we played, the tighter we got and the better the songs became. Drugs, of course, were a by-product of being on the road, but I also saw first-hand just how detrimental they could be. I came across many people of undoubted talent, but it was obvious they had been fucked up by cocaine, or else heroin. Touring *Obsession*, we did quite a few shows with Aerosmith, who were the biggest band in America at the time. I expected them to be a devastating live band, but they were so out of it by then that songs would virtually grind to a halt and the crowd would go quiet. That happened at every show. They were supposed to be America's Rolling Stones, but it was us that went out and grabbed their audience by the balls. That's what would happen if you weren't 100 per cent fit as a band and able to do the business – someone else would come along and steal your thunder. And with the world at our feet, I was still focused on my main goal. For all the drugs, the biggest high I got back then was from my band having an album in the charts and playing to thousands of people a night.

CHAPTER 7

*In which a cruel twist of fate snatches defeat from the jaws
of victory, as a prelude to our intrepid hero fearing
his nose is about to fall off.*

———

Once our tour budget was relaxed, we were able to bring
our wives and girlfriends out on the road with us for periods
of time. It helped to slow down some of our nocturnal
activities, but to be honest even that got to be a drag. If
Jo joined me for, say, three weeks, I'd actually be relieved
when she went home again. That sounds terrible, I know,
but on the road I existed in a complete bubble from inside
which it required a huge effort to maintain anything like
a normal relationship. There was, too, the simple fact that
I would have to supress my urges and not be the *real* me.
See, the band was my gang, even my surrogate family. If I
turned to anyone for advice it would be to Phil, before and
above another soul. And I didn't allow wives or girlfriends
to come between us.

In an interlude between an American and UK tour, though, the band flew back to England and Jo and I got married in Essex, where she was brought up and her family still lived. From my perspective, the two of us had been quite happily ticking along and I'd not felt the need for us to be man and wife. But Jo decided that she wanted to start a family and be traditional about it. It was a summer wedding, but more low-key than when I'd got married to Yvonne – a registry office affair.

Neill Way: Pete and Josephine were married at Wanstead Registry Office that summer. I had just then started a new job and it was such a last-minute affair that more or less in my first week I had to ask for time off to attend. As you might imagine, my new boss was incredulous that I hadn't known earlier about my brother getting married but that was Pete for you.

Ross Halfin: I'll tell you one of the funniest stories I ever heard about Pete. A few days after Pete's wedding, UFO did a gig at the Roundhouse in Camden. Andy Parker was the first of them to turn up at the venue and told Wilf Wright that he'd heard a rumour that Pete had gone and got married. When Pete arrived on the scene, Wilf pulled him to one side and asked him if it was true. 'Well, yeah,' said Pete. 'But Pete,' Wilf pointed out, 'you haven't even got your divorce through from Yvonne.' From what I heard, Jo had given Pete an ultimatum that she was going to leave him if he didn't marry her, so he went ahead with the wedding regardless of still being hitched to Yvonne.

No, that's one story at least that isn't correct. Yvonne and I *had* got divorced. The thing was that I had no idea where Yvonne was living with baby Zowie and no means of getting in touch, so I didn't have the actual divorce certificate on me. Bloody hell, I've done more than a few stupid things in my time, but to risk going to jail for bigamy wasn't one of them.

There wasn't the time for a honeymoon: we had the UK shows to play and then were back out on the road again in America. We had also decided to capitalize on our success by making a live album. Back then, that was what you did if you were a major band – the double live record was seen as a sort of status symbol. Ron Nevison and Mike Clink came out to join us in Chicago and Louisville, and recorded three or four shows using the Record Plant mobile. Ron taped a couple of smaller shows at the Gardens in Louisville, which thirty-eight years later was where the public funeral service was held for Muhammad Ali, and then a night at the Chicago International Amphitheatre in front of 12,000 or so people. Then, when Ron and Mike went back to LA to mix the tapes, all of us in the band would go down to the studio every day just in case they needed anything fixing. But there was very little that needed to be done. Michael re-did some of his parts, but then, Michael was very fussy. As a whole, though, *Strangers in the Night* ended up being a very representative live album; it really was like listening to us play onstage every night. It was our audience that you hear on there, too, not like Thin Lizzy's *Live and Dangerous,* which came out that year. Lizzy could only play small club shows in the States, so they used the sound of a David Bowie crowd on their record.

Mike Clink: Ron and I had just finished up making a record with the Babys and literally the next morning, I was on a flight to Chicago to get everything set up for UFO. We actually recorded ten shows over a period of a couple of weeks, mostly club gigs but also some big arena shows in Chicago and Lexington, Kentucky. Even so, I never got tired of seeing them play. They were an amazing live band. You couldn't really compare the way the two bands sounded, but UFO certainly had the same sort of energy onstage as Guns N' Roses had when I first saw them.

Pete was always flying across the stage, putting the headstock of his bass in people's faces. His rapport with the audience was fantastic. Now, during the live shows, he and the rest of the band were certainly more inebriated than they would be in the studio, but it made for a great performance. To this day, I still have people come up and tell me that it's one of the two or three greatest live records ever made by a rock band.

By that point, though, we'd been on the road pretty much non-stop for three years and there was no question we were all burnt out. Towards the end of the *Obsession* tour, we had begun to travel to and from the shows in separate cars, which kept a lid on most things. However, there was a big falling-out between Phil and Michael. I wasn't there at the time, but the account I've most commonly heard is that Phil ended up punching Michael. I do know the two of them had a heated discussion over Mandrax, because, I believe, Michael had taken the last pill.

Michael came to speak to me later that same evening and told me that he never wanted to play with Phil again. He was, though, back on the bus again the next day, but when Michael held a grudge, he wouldn't let it go. For ever afterwards, he and Phil didn't see eye to eye on anything, which was particularly trying for me because I got on perfectly well with the pair of them. In between encores, I'd be stood at the side of the stage and have Michael saying to me, 'For me, Phil is an arsehole.' No sooner would Michael have walked off than Phil would sidle over and ask me, 'How is that German cunt, then?'

I think most of all Michael resented Phil's leadership of the band and from that point on he kind of distanced himself from the rest of us. He would stay out of band meetings, assuming that it would be Phil who would make all the decisions. Apart from one particular occasion, that is, when Michael cracked and shouted at Phil, 'You think you are the Führer!' That was quite amusing, even though I don't think Phil took any notice.

The rest of us in the band tried not to have conversations on the subject of Michael. We thought that if we kept quiet about it, all the problems would somehow go away. And it wasn't as if we were all miserable *all* the time, far from it, but there was a certain pervasive atmosphere – most apparent after we had all been on the booze. By the end of the tour, it had reached the point where being in UFO was like going to a wedding in which two sides of the same family all get drunk and start rowing.

It was once we got back to LA and were tidying up *Strangers in the Night* that things came to a head. Michael very clearly wasn't happy. He got particularly bent out of shape with Ron over the version of 'Rock Bottom' that ended up on the album, but, in general, he retreated into his shell. It just so happened that, at the same time, Joe Perry had walked out on Aerosmith. I'd often noticed Steven Tyler watching us from the side of the stage when we'd played with Aerosmith, so it wasn't exactly a surprise that he got their manager to call Wilf to see if Michael would be allowed to go and rehearse with them, with a view to him replacing Joe. Michael flew up to Aerosmith's hometown of Boston and seemed pretty much straight away to have talked himself out of the job. From what I heard, he told Steven he should come down off his high horse, which wouldn't have been received very well.

Whatever did happen, Michael was put on a plane to London the next day and that was it for him with Aerosmith and also with us. The next thing we heard, he'd gone off to make a solo record for Chrysalis. That ended up being delayed, though, apparently by Michael having a bit of a breakdown. I believe he shaved off all of his hair and ran off to Belgium for some reason. Actually, he left three bands in almost one go, because not long after that he re-joined the Scorpions to play on their *Lovedrive* album and then walked out on them again, too.

I can laugh about it now, but it was a huge blow for us losing Michael, especially so just then. It was as if we'd climbed all the way up the mountain and were about to summit, only to have the ground give way beneath our feet. But then, with Michael anything was possible. His behaviour could be baffling, maddening, but that sort of volatile chemistry had given us an extra edge. Unfortunately, it also helped to destroy the band. To put it in football terms, we'd made it all the way to the Cup Final and then our star player had quit the team on the eve of the big game.

Michael Schenker: *For me, it is all based on intuitive decision making. From the time I was seventeen, I've not known what I was doing but acted on intuition. I think perhaps I look at life in a different way to other people.*

Ross Halfin: *You didn't realize how good Schenker was and what an important part of their sound he'd been until he left. If Schenker had* *stayed with them, UFO would have been right up there with AC/DC in terms of being a legendary band. The problem for Schenker, though, was Phil Mogg. Schenker couldn't really speak English and was a bit of an oddball to be honest, but Phil would just take the piss out of him all of the time. They all did, but Phil was quite vindictive and nasty about it. Michael was crazy in his own way, but Phil was why he upped and left. They were on the verge of a huge breakthrough in America, too. That's the real tragedy of UFO and they're the great lost British rock band in that respect.*

———

The immediate aftermath of Michael's abrupt departure was a difficult period, but also surreal for us. The record label threw us a huge party to launch the live album at the Griffith Park Observatory, right up in the hills overlooking Hollywood. I suppose it was all very lavish, but I just wasn't in the mood to celebrate. Quite frankly, I'd have been happier if it had been held at a crack house. I'd certainly have preferred that to a buffet and cake.

There was, at least, some light relief. It was a sign of our new standing that a member of UFO was asked to appear on a special music edition of NBC TV's long-running quiz show, *Hollywood Squares*. The show was like a glorified version of noughts and crosses and for some reason unfeasibly popular. Phil was originally supposed to do it, but couldn't be arsed, so Wilf press-ganged me into taking his place instead. In return, I managed to coerce Wilf into getting me a limo out to the NBC studios in Burbank and ensuring there were plentiful supplies of Jack Daniel's and cocaine in my dressing room.

Besides me, there was a motley collection of other guests, among them Chaka Khan, Todd Rundgren, Kiki Dee and KC from the Sunshine Band. The whole day was bloody hilarious, actually. They billed me as 'Mr UFO', and the host, Peter Marshall, who'd been doing the show since it began in 1966, very obviously hadn't the first clue about who I was. But then, he did dress like my dad. I even managed to get a couple of questions right, and between takes would duck under my desk and take a big snort from a bag of coke, or else share a slug of Jack with Kiki Dee.

Chrysalis rush-released *Strangers in the Night* in January 1979, because they were so desperate to get us back on the road. Soon enough, half the world was telling us it was one of the best live albums ever recorded. It rocketed into the *Billboard* chart in America and also went Top 10 back home in the UK. That really brought all of those songs to the attention of people who hadn't heard them before. All of a sudden, a song such as 'Doctor Doctor', which up till then hadn't had any sort of status, became a must-have item in our set. People started to complain if we didn't play it. And years later, I would read interviews with people like Slash from Guns N' Roses, saying how he'd learned to play guitar to *Strangers in the Night*.

In America, we went out and did the same arenas we'd just done on the back of *Obsession*, and to huge crowds. This time, though, the success was bittersweet. We had fulfilled our biggest ambition, which was to break through in the US, but it was as though we weren't really able to exploit it. To replace Michael, we'd had to bring Paul Chapman back in at short notice. Paul fitted in really well, as if he hadn't been away in fact, but people had bought a live album with Michael on it and now he wasn't there.

A few years later, I bumped into Eddie Van Halen in Seattle and spent a day off with him doing the usual things. Eddie told me that when Michael had left, he'd wanted to audition for UFO but didn't feel confident enough to call us. That would have been interesting to say the least, Eddie Van Halen in UFO, but it was not to be.

Ross Halfin: I saw them with Paul Chapman, not long after Schenker had left. They were doing Long Beach Arena in LA and were amazing. But there was a guy stood on the front row, he had a scarf pulled down over his eyes, and all through the gig he held up a cardboard sign with Schenker's name on it.

We did three months of straight touring in America, co-headlining with AC/DC at first and then with Judas Priest opening up for us. Going out with AC/DC in particular was great, because we always got a kick from putting ourselves up in competition against a really good band. They had just then released their *Highway to Hell* album, so were right at the top of their game. They were also typical, down-to-earth Australian blokes. In fact, one of the ways for you to guarantee falling foul of them was to have any airs or graces. On the opening leg of the tour, Angus and Malcolm Young were sharing a room. The first time I popped down to see them, the pair of them were propped up in their beds like two old men. Angus was just twenty-three or twenty-four at the time, and Mal not much older, but there on their bedside table were two glasses of water with false teeth submerged in them. They came a long way from that point, that's for sure. Mal was terrific, but a hard man too. Angus once told me that his brother had his guitar strings made out of barbed wire. Oftentimes, Mal would get into a fight in a bar. Some bloke would call him Shorty or something like that, and Mal would never back down, not even with family. Very early in the tour, we did a club show together and as they came offstage after their set, Mal and Angus suddenly went at it with each other. The two of them were rolling around together on the floor, trading punches. Then they got back up, dusted themselves down and went out to do an encore as if nothing had happened. Apparently, even years later they would come to blows for no apparent reason. It broke my heart to hear of Malcolm's illness and the fact that he cannot now even remember being in the band.

I got on especially well with Angus. After every show, I'd go and have a drink in his room at the hotel or else he'd come up to mine. The only thing Angus ever had in his room was his Gibson SG guitar. It wouldn't have surprised me if he'd have even slept with it. One night, the two of us were in my room and I pulled out a stash of coke that I'd hidden under the bureau. I always felt a bit funny doing coke in front of Angus, because all that he ever wanted was a cup of tea, but I did chop out a couple of lines. Angus peered over at me and said, 'Here, Pete, you want to get yourself a good breakfast instead of that stuff.' He was a bright bloke, Angus.

Angus didn't actually mind what you got up to, but then he was used to being around Mal and AC/DC's singer, Bon Scott. Those two were hardly shy and retiring types. I got to know Bon very well, and he was otherwise one of the nicest, most laid-back people I've met. Nothing ever seemed to get on his nerves and you could talk to him about absolutely anything at all. There wasn't an aggressive bone in Bon's body, but his personality was larger than life. What you saw with Bon was what you got. He'd only ever wear jeans, a T-shirt, a leather jacket on occasion, or else be bare-chested, but nothing more than that, and there was always a twinkle in his eye. The words he wrote to all of those classic AC/DC songs pretty much described him to a tee. Each evening, just before the tour bus left for the venue, he would come down from his hotel room, walk straight from the lift to the bar, and knock back a double Jack Daniel's. And almost without fail, he'd announce that he'd had a good workout the night before with some girl or other. Angus used to say to me, 'You know, Bon's been drunk three times today.' What he meant was, Bon had been on a bender, gone back to his bunk on the bus, got up again, had another round of drinks, and then repeated the cycle. I think Angus had concluded that the sleeping interludes were the only sober parts of Bon's day. But Bon loved what he was doing and enjoyed himself to the full, it was that simple.

We sold out a couple of nights at Long Beach Arena. Even though these were hometown shows for UFO, I rented a suite at the Sunset Marquis just for the occasion. At that time, Bob Geldof and the Boomtown Rats were the big things in the British music press and they were also in town, but to do a club gig. Every hour of the day, Paula Yates, Bob's then-girlfriend, would sunbathe by the pool, which was directly outside of my room. Eventually, the two of us struck up a conversation and got along very well. In no time, she had asked me to pose for a book that she was doing, *Rock Stars in their Underpants*. I was game for anything and we ended up doing the photographs in my suite. Bob came along with

Paula. I had a load of coke piled up on the table to help get me in the mood, and then stripped down to just my pants and a *Dawn of the Dead* horror movie T-shirt. I never did get to see the finished book, but I ran into Paula here and there a few times after that, and she was always lovely. The tour we did with Judas Priest was good, too. In particular, I spent a lot of time hanging out with their guitarist, Glenn Tipton, who was quite a boy, shall we say. He was my sort of person in other words. Priest's singer, Rob Halford, used to tell the pair of us that it was the ones who stayed up all night who ruined it for everyone else the next day. Halford is a lovely guy, but it was always likely that you would have to make excuses for him. I think Rob's sexuality is well known, and many was the time I was in a hotel coffee shop or bar and one or other of Rob's boyfriends would turn up and be hysterical. Literally, these guys would weep to me about not being able to get hold of Rob and beg of me, 'Can you call and tell him Angel Fingers is here?'

——

There was a monumental day on that tour when our accountant told us that we could write off our drugs against medical expenses. He claimed to have heard that Emerson, Lake and Palmer used to do the same thing. It was doubtless an urban myth, or else he was desperately trying to be one of the boys, but, nevertheless, to us, it was like a red rag to a bull. A couple of months later, the poor guy nearly had a heart attack when he realized we'd run up a $20,000 medical bill, which was a small fortune in those days, and the lot of it on coke.

In general, I spent my money just as fast as I earned it. I mean, we were playing to a load of people every night – one month we were even listed in *Billboard* magazine as one of the top-grossing live acts in America – so I assumed we must be making a load of money too. I never even looked at my bank account. Eventually, though, even I started to wonder where all of that cash was going. Our accounting procedures had always been something of a mystery to me, but I should perhaps have realized that the situation wasn't quite as reliable as I'd assumed.

We did have high expenses as well. If we had to fly, we made sure we were sat at the front of the plane, and we had a policy of only staying in five-star hotels. Being on the road for the amount of time we were, we wanted our luxuries, and it wasn't as if we weren't earning them. And for as long as we kept rolling on, I was happy in my ignorance. Like an idiot, it was only when the money ran out that I began to question things.

One of the pleasures I would look forward to most was going back to play in the UK. I got increasingly worn down from trooping around America, whereas in Britain you had a whole different culture with regard to the fans. There wasn't the thing with groupies, or at least not to anywhere near the same extent. That being said, I still had the same number of drug dealers turn up. In fact, we re-christened the *Strangers in the Night* UK tour the 'Tapping the Tables Tour'. Every night, I would end up frantically doing all these deep-breathing exercises to try and slow my heart rate down. Next morning, I'd walk onto the tour bus like a shellshock victim. It got to the point where my nose bled all of the time. Our schedule, though, was relentless, unforgiving. I was looking at one of our old itineraries the other day and one UK tour alone ran for two months, with just a couple of days off in between the shows. That was the problem: when you were hot in those days you had to be out there in front of people – no matter how exhausted you were and even if your nose might be about to fall off.

CHAPTER 8

*In which the death of Bon Scott is reflected upon and
paternal thoughts are offered on the subject of doing
hard drugs in front of one's children.*

———

Neill Way: *Pete and Josephine came back to live in England just in
time for my wedding in 1979. In fact, they literally came to the church
from the airport. Jo was pregnant at the time, but to me that day was
more typical of the mess that Pete used to trail around with him. The
airline had lost most of their luggage in transit and so Pete turned up at
the church resplendent in an especially bright and flowery shirt. He was,
in fact, wearing one of Jo's blouses.*

At the end of the *Strangers in the Night* tour, there had been
a consensus in the band that we should move back home. In
the event, though, it was only Phil, Paul Chapman and I who
returned to England while Paul Raymond and Andy stayed
on in LA. That distance between us in miles was soon enough
being felt on a personal level, too, and it would eventually pull

us apart. For now, though, Jo and I rented a place out in Kew, useful for me as it was close to Heathrow Airport. Not long after we moved in, our daughter Charlotte was born. It was good timing for me, since we weren't on tour and I didn't have to cancel any shows. I was there for Charlotte's birth, though the thing I remember most about it was wondering how long it was all going to take. Not that I didn't change my share of nappies while we were in Kew. In fact, changing nappies is my abiding memory of bringing up babies. That and not doing drugs or being drunk in front of them. As I can testify all too well, they soon grow up sufficiently to be able to ask Mummy, 'Is Daddy all right?' It would be fair to say I was an erratic father, but not a beast. For the most part, I felt like I was being a responsible parent by working hard to make the band popular and keep the money coming in. But then, I wasn't much use at doing anything else.

As a family, the three of us lived comfortably because of my efforts. But no sooner would I have to leave to go on tour again than I would succumb once more to temptation. There was never a question of my being true to my marital vows. I had a loving wife and child at home in England, but then would have the most beautiful girl in all of, say, Chicago promise me undying love. It was all but impossible for me to resist, and though I would feel guilty and remorseful, within the framework of the band it was just the way things were. The truth of the matter is that the dream you have when you start a band is that you might one day be rich, and the pursuit of that goal defines everything about the way you think and act. Sometimes a wife or girlfriend can become secondary to that vision. Ultimately, I had a job that I loved, and nothing or no one was going to get in the way of me doing it. I believed the best I could do was to make sure my wife and child also enjoyed the fruits of my labour.

Jo, Charlotte and I eventually moved to Twickenham. I bought us a terraced house on a very nice street. Our neighbours were accountants, solicitors and the like, so, of course, I stood out like a sore thumb. To be truthful, I was never able to adjust to family life. I tried to fit into its routines, but I'm pretty sure that each of my wives thought of me more as a child than a husband. Josephine certainly treated me like a boy and we'd only just then had a baby together. I quite liked to cook when I was at home, but I left almost everything else around the house to Jo.

At the same time, by then I'd brought a particular aspect of my work home with me. I was regularly doing coke and also occasionally snorting heroin in the house. I did make a conscious effort not to let my escalating drug use get in the way of family affairs, such as mealtimes, but I spent most of the rest of my time zonked out in front of the telly, or else would go into town to see a band. That was the irony of my life: I was exhausted from being on the road, but couldn't function off it.

Strangers in the Night had been the band's biggest success, but it proved to be double-edged. From that point on, Chrysalis pushed for us to write a hit single. Up till then we had been steadily selling albums, but hadn't had the sort of big breakthrough song that bands such as Foreigner – with 'Cold as Ice' – and Journey – with 'Lovin', Touchin', Squeezin'' – were starting to get in America. We hadn't written specific singles either, and as a result the ones that we had released to that point had been almost completely overlooked. Chrysalis hit

117

upon the bright idea of getting the legendary George Martin in to produce our next record. In their thinking, since George had done it with the Beatles, he was bound to be able to coerce us into conjuring up a proper pop tune. In theory it was a smart enough strategy, but for the fact that our idea of what a pop song should sound like wasn't akin to the Beatles so much as to the Who in their earliest days, and needed to have that kind of power and fury. Taking that into account, things were perhaps always likely to go wrong between George and us.

Nevertheless, George came down to meet us at rehearsals and didn't have to try too hard to convince us to make our next record, *No Place to Run*, at his studio on the Caribbean island of Montserrat. We also got the services of Geoff Emerick, George's engineer, which meant that the two blokes who'd recorded *Sgt. Pepper's Lonely Hearts Club Band* were now on our team. Although, in our case neither of them was given the slightest chance either to use a sitar or to bring in string arrangements.

Montserrat itself was very colonial feeling, like a living museum of the British Empire. Paul Chapman, Andy and I even stayed in an old colonial house just up the road from the studio. We had butlers, maids and kitchen staff. Phil, Paul Raymond and their older children were off in another house, but all of us brought our wives and girlfriends out with us. Apart from childcare, pretty much all that Jo had to do for a month was sit around the pool all day. George was also very old-school English, an absolute gentleman. He had his studio manned by a black staff, all of whom had to dress in crisp white uniforms. Dinner was always served at 6 p.m., which was when George would allow himself his gin and tonic. For better or worse, the whole experience was like being on an extended holiday. You could run out from the studio doors and jump straight into the pool. And while I didn't have any coke with me on the island, the local rum was an especially potent beverage. I did on occasion get a little worse for wear, but George was very accommodating of our behaviour in that respect. In contrast to me at least, George was very fit. He would go down to the beach each morning and swim three miles round to a cove and back.

The studio itself was a very well-appointed set-up – the Stones and the Police had both worked there in the recent past. George would always want us to get off to an early start – by 11 a.m. at the latest. Even for us, that wasn't too hard since we would wake up each morning to glorious sunshine. Our priority, on the other hand, was to make sure that the studio bar was well stocked. And a running theme of the sessions would be for George very politely to ask the rest of us where Phil had disappeared to and how he was getting on with his lyrics. On most occasions, Phil would actually have wandered down to the beach for a paddle, or else have gone out water-skiing. I think it's true to say that George was more completely bemused by Phil than by any of us. He told us that he had never before worked with a band that would put down backing tracks without having heard any vocals. For our part, it soon became worryingly apparent that George preferred to have the tracks sound too placid, or muted, for our tastes. The second he and Geoff ever left the room, we would rush to turn them up. It's a wonder we didn't blow the roof off.

In the end, we spent a month on Montserrat and didn't manage to get any of the vocals done. Phil simply never got around to finishing his lyrics. George was reduced to going on to us about how when he had worked with the Beatles, Paul McCartney and John Lennon or else George Harrison would always sing him a complete song before they recorded it. Rhetorically, he would ask how a record could ever be accomplished otherwise. George's mounting frustration aside, I think he liked the fact that we were a rock band, something different for him. For us, though, there was none of the fun and games that we'd had with Ron Nevison, nor were the end results as good.

A few years later, I bumped into George strolling along Oxford Street one afternoon. As ever, he was very gracious: 'Hello, Peter. How are you and what have you been up to?' That's how I remember him being: well mannered, well meaning and a thoroughly decent man. Unfortunately, he mastered the *No Place to Run* album so that it was more low-key and restrained sounding than we wanted and needed it to be. George gave it the polished studio sound of a pop band, which I guess was also what Chrysalis would have been anticipating.

We did, at least, get to do *Top of the Pops* for the first time when the album's lead-off single, 'Young Blood', briefly threatened to storm the UK charts. That was something of a landmark, since we'd all of us grown up watching *Top of the Pops*. Being on it, at that time, was still enough to convince your mum and dad that you had got a proper job. We went on to make two or three appearances on the show, but in reality it was a bit of a nuisance to do. It was meant to appear as if you were performing live, so you would have to take a day out in order to troop along to the BBC studio in Barnes, supposedly to re-record your track. A guy from the Musicians Union would also turn up to oversee the session, but instead would go off down the pub. We'd sit around twiddling our thumbs for an hour, and when the union guy returned, the BBC engineer would hand him a tape of the track that he'd just then run off from our album. Apparently, no one would ever bother to re-cut their song.

It took another day for you to film your slot, which was also pretty boring. It was like being stood on a factory production line: you waited hours for your turn, did your bit, did it again and then went home. There was never a reason to hang about the place, especially since we weren't allowed near the show's dance troupe, Legs & Co. A fat lot of good it did us, too. The week after we appeared on *Top of the Pops*, 'Young Blood' dropped like a stone in the charts.

———

Until we played it live, *No Place to Run* never sounded right to me. Some of the reviews rightly said that the album came across as limp, so we set out on tour determined to prove that there was more to it than that. Paul Chapman was by that point like a fish to water, so we were in great shape as a band. On this occasion, we kicked off by touring the UK, and our run of dates peaked with a four-night stand at the famous Hammersmith Odeon, which had become like a second home to us. The Odeon was a great place to play, since it was a classically big hall but much more intimate than an arena. Often as not though, we had to work harder to win over our hometown crowd and got a wilder response at places like Glasgow Apollo or Newcastle City Hall. The shows we did at those venues are some of the best I can remember.

Joe Elliott: UFO came to do Sheffield City Hall on the No Place to Run tour. I went backstage and met up with Pete. He was very pleasant, polite and exactly how I expected him to be, this sort of cocky Cockney geezer. He liked to play the fey, Carnaby Street 1968 vintage rogue and he would have been perfect in the Stones, the Kinks or the Small Faces because those are the bands he would rattle on about all night. In fact, if you threw Keith Richards and Ronnie Wood in a bucket and mixed them up, you'd end up with Pete.

He was starving after the gig and wanted to go out and get something to eat. It was midnight by then and in those days there weren't exactly twenty-four-hour restaurants everywhere. There was, though, this kind of hole-in-the-wall fast-food joint where taxi drivers and other night workers used to go for a bacon sandwich and which was built into the arch of an old railway tunnel.

I took Pete over there and we lined up in a queue alongside all these cabbies and also a group of hardcore bikers. The two of us were both wearing Capezios and tight black plastic trousers, and Pete also had on a fake leopard-skin coat and mascara. At one point, he turned to me and said, 'Here, why is everybody looking at us?' I mean, duh!

Not too long after that, I moved to Isleworth, which wasn't far from where Pete was living in Twickenham, and the two of us ended up becoming drinking buddies. I was quite shocked when I first went round to Pete's house. I mean to say, it was tiny. I figured that all rock stars lived in mansions, but there he was in this terraced house. Charlotte would have been a year or so old at the time. I remember babysitting her once while Pete and Jo buggered off somewhere. Most of the time, Pete and I would be in one room with our beers and fish and chips, listening to music, and Jo would be in the kitchen, or else putting Charlotte to bed. The two of them seemed to have a good relationship, though it did appear to be founded on sarcasm. There was a lot of, 'What the fuck

are you going on about?' It was good-natured, though, and also there
weren't a lot of drugs going off with Pete, or at least that I could see.
It was only later in life that I really saw what he was capable of.

Our last Hammersmith show on that tour was on 7 February
1980. I remember the exact date because Bon Scott came down
to see us. He was in town to write songs for what turned out
to be AC/DC's *Back in Black* album, though I don't suppose it
was called that at the time. Ross Halfin took a picture of us that
night, having a drink together backstage. Neither of us looks
fucked up in the slightest in that photograph, but it's the last
known one there is of Bon alive. Twelve days later, he was dead.

Ever since then, a sort of conspiracy theory has grown up that
I hooked Bon up with drugs and that this led him to his death.
The truth is that I never saw him again after that Hammersmith
show. I might well have had heroin on me that night, but I
certainly didn't offer it to him. Heroin is something you tend to
keep quiet and to yourself, and is not a social drug like cocaine.
And I even used to keep cocaine to myself, because I just wasn't
one for sharing my drugs. There was an Australian guy with
Bon at the Odeon and I do know for a fact that he would have
had drugs on him, because he was also a friend of mine and
essentially a dealer. However, Bon seemed perfectly lucid to
me. The two of us were good friends, but it was only small
talk that passed between us that night. 'How are you? What
are you up to? Fancy a drink some time?' – that sort of thing.
Bon hung out for an hour or so in our dressing room and then
around midnight went off with this other guy. That was the last
time I saw him. Bon and I may well have made plans to meet
up again in the days ahead, but we never got around to it. It was

almost two weeks later, when I got a call at home late one night from Paul Chapman. From what I've been able to gather since, another acquaintance had been out with Bon on that particular night and called Paul first to tell him the terrible news. This guy told Paul that he and Bon had been out drinking and that afterwards he'd driven Bon back to his flat, and then left him passed out in the back of his car on the road outside. At some point during the night, Bon had thrown up in his sleep and choked on his own vomit.

It was Paul who told me that Bon was dead. He asked me if I had a number for Angus or Malcolm, because no one had been able to get hold of them. I gave Paul Mal's number and I called Angus later the same day to say how sorry I was to have heard about Bon. That was an awfully sad, grim conversation. Angus was in a terrible state. He told me that he had still got some of Bon's stuff in his flat waiting for him to collect it.

Nobody since then, including the coroner in his report, has ever said publicly that there were drugs in Bon's system that night. However, I've always believed there must have been more to his death than him having drunk too much. I realize that Bon was reported to have downed seven double whiskeys that night, but he didn't have any limits with alcohol from what I saw. I mean, I never knew him be unable to stand or function, no matter how much he'd happened to have put away at a time. I still find it quite unbelievable that for somebody who could drink as much as Bon did, it was alcohol alone that caused him to vomit. Oftentimes, I saw him drink a bar dry and then go to sleep back at the hotel or on the bus without any trouble whatsoever.

I think it's possible that Bon did use heroin that night. It's a well-known fact that if you take heroin, it will make you throw up and possibly also pass out. Taken in the situation that Bon was in, with booze also involved, you would need to get up and walk around, because your heart rate would have quite considerably slowed down. Someone who used on a regular basis would have known to be careful, particularly when mixing with alcohol. To my knowledge, Bon wasn't a regular user of hard drugs. It's only my opinion, but I think it's at least probable that he sniffed some heroin that night and then passed out. And I think that's what caused him to choke, even though it never came up in the autopsy.

By the time of Bon's funeral, we were back out on tour, so I couldn't attend the service. What else can I say but that it was an awful thing to have happened and that I still miss him? In respect of my own drug use, though, it wasn't as if Bon's death was like an alarm call to me, not at all. For one thing, I wasn't yet an addict, or so I believed. And I continued to be drawn to heroin, just as I was to cocaine, or booze, or to any other drug that was made available to me. That was the kind of person I was, simple as that.

To be honest, I also believed that I knew how to handle heroin. I wouldn't have a big blowout, but took it in smaller, more manageable quantities just to keep a momentum going. I thought I was being careful with it, responsible if you like. Of course, what had happened to Bon did cross my mind from time to time, but I believed I was in control of my drug taking and not the other way round. Stupidly, I was also still very self-confident concerning my tolerance for drugs. As fate would have it, I'd just then found a perfect partner in crime from within the band. Paul Chapman was a very good guitarist, but much more of a Jack the Lad than Michael had ever been. To my mind, Paul was a kind of market trader, because he was always up to scams and would have talked you into some dodgy deal or other before you knew it, quite often involving illegal narcotics. There was something of the Artful Dodger about the way he looked, too, with his unkempt hair and almost bashful grin. Soon enough, the rest of us in the band started to call him Tonka, after the well-known toys, since Paul also seemed to be indestructible. In particular, his capacity for all of the things you shouldn't take was enormous and apparently boundless.

There was nothing that Paul wouldn't do to a ridiculous level. For instance, he would think nothing of nicking a guitar from out of the window of a music shop in the middle of the night, just because he fancied having a play. Or else he would be found roaming the streets of, say, Hamburg at daybreak, in a tired and emotional state. I don't want to say he was like a breath of fresh air after Michael, but it was nice to have someone so carefree in the band. The two of us had an awful lot of fun together after shows, be it in hotel bars or up in our rooms, when the mirror would inevitably come out. One time, Paul went off to Kensington Market and bought himself a very expensive pair of bespoke, hand-made leather boots for a tour to Germany. The first show we did was at a sports hall which had an Olympic-sized swimming pool. After the gig, I went down to check out the pool and there was a girl in the water, completely naked. The next thing I saw was Paul's boots bubbling up to the surface and floating by – completely ruined. They had clearly paid the price for Paul's haste to get his rocks off. But that was typical of Paul. He acted first and thought later, if at all. It really is no wonder we got along so well.

——

By the time we got off the road, our other Paul had been booted out of the band. The decision was out of my hands, but from what I gathered either or both of Phil and Wilf had got fed up with Paul's abrasive manner. At all events, he'd said something untoward to one or the other of them, which wasn't unusual for him, and that had proved to be the final straw for them. As luck would have it, Michael was just then looking for a guitarist and keyboard player and still signed to Chrysalis, so Paul walked straight out of our band and into his.

Paul's departure barely interrupted our schedule. No sooner had he gone than we had recruited a replacement, Neil Carter, who had been playing in a band called Wild Horses with ex-Rainbow bassist Jimmy Bain and the former Thin Lizzy guitarist Brian Robertson. Neil was a nice bloke and talented musician, but he didn't half do my head in at times. He used to breed cats and while I'd be grabbing bottles of vodka off the drinks trolley on a flight, he'd be sat there reading up on the genetic strengths of Persians and Siamese in *Cat Monthly*. I can't say I wasn't forewarned, though. The late, great Jimmy Bain had told me that when he had originally called to offer Neil the gig in Wild Horses, Neil's mother had answered the phone. She informed Jimmy that Neil was out in the garden tending to the roses. Now, Jimmy was a tough Scot and he and Brian were so volatile together that they were known as Nitro and Glycerine. When Neil finally did come to the phone, Jimmy told him straight: 'When yer in Wild Horses, ye'll nae be doing the fucking flowers, son.'

127

That was just the beginning of the odd stories we got to hear about Neil. When we first went out on the road with him, a girl who claimed to have been up in his room told me that she'd found women's clothes and high heels hidden away in his wardrobe. It was true enough that Neil was quite effeminate, but he had a girlfriend at the time and so I presumed that they must have belonged to her. When Neil finally left the band, he did actually come out as gay. And every year after that, Phil would get a very nice Christmas card from Neil and his boyfriend.

The first major show we did with Neil was as headliners of the Reading Festival in August 1980. We played to a 40,000-plus crowd and Wilf had done a deal whereby we got a percentage of the gate money, which turned out to be considerably more than the appearance fee we were originally offered. Not that we saw much of it. We were still paying off Chrysalis for our first four American tours, not to mention everything else. In no other respect was that our most glorious gig either. A young, hungry Iron Maiden had gone on right before us and taken the place by storm. It was also quite late by the time we took to the stage, which didn't work to our advantage. By then, we had been sat in our trailer for several hours along with a great pile of booze, about which no more need be said. After Reading, we went back into the studio and got on with our next album, *The Wild, the Willing and the Innocent*. To this day, it's one of my favourite records of ours – the perfect combination of hard rock and melody, and interesting to me for having some really good ballads on it such as 'Profession of Violence'. We recorded it at Air Studios on Oxford Street and those sessions had their moments. To begin with, for example, I was using a fleet of cab drivers to ferry to the studio packets of 'goodies' hidden in cassette boxes. It soon turned out that one of them was an undercover reporter for the *News of the World* newspaper. Two weeks into our residency, the paper ran a big story about a huge drug bust in London, which just happened to have been at the exact same premises as my drivers were going along to.

Drug dealers were invaluable people to know, but dangerous to fall out with. There was one occasion when someone in the band's circle thought he might make a tidy profit from selling on an ounce of coke. However, he ended up snorting the lot, before he had paid for it. Since the bloke he had bought it from then got banged up in jail, though, he assumed he was off the hook. Until, that is, the phone in his flat started to ring every day at 3 a.m. and an unidentified but menacing male voice would tell him that they knew where he lived. For the next three weeks, he stayed home with all of the lights off.

The Wild, the Willing and the Innocent was released at the start of 1981 and we set off behind it on a coast-to-coast tour of America with Cheap Trick. I got Jo to come out for a spell and bring Charlotte along with her, and imagined being able to make it like a family holiday for the pair of them. To be honest, though, the reality was that their presence on the road made hardly any difference to my now well-established tour routine, and I spent most of the time holed up in hotel rooms doing lines of coke. It was incredibly selfish of me, but I just assumed that Jo would be fine so long as there were other wives and girlfriends around and someone for Charlotte to play with.

Pete Makowski: *The thing was UFO had all the accoutrements that the really huge rock bands had, like incredibly glamorous wives and girlfriends, but never the money. I flew out to San Francisco to* *see them do a Day of the Green show in July 1981. They played to a vast, enthusiastic crowd, which in hindsight gave me an idea as to just how big they could have gone on to become. However, it was also on that trip that I realized that chaos had by now surrounded Pete and the band. For just one thing, a guy from their crew was charged with procuring all of their drugs for the tour. He turned up one afternoon at the hotel and Pete thought it would be a great prank to throw him in the pool. In the guy went, but with three months' supplies of cocaine on his person.*

Like a lot of addictive people, Pete is very charming and also extremely vulnerable. He is a man-child in that sense, though I know that people close to him such as Josephine and Charlotte must have suffered terribly as a result. He's caused an unbelievable amount of carnage and I'm sure that must have registered with him somehow. Whenever I met up with Pete, I'd either end up going off with him on some insane adventure, or else he would just vanish for a couple of days. And if you were with him, having a laugh, and Jo happened to walk into the room, you could not help but feel guilty. I actually used to go and visit the pair of them with my son, who would play with Charlotte. I went upstairs to Pete's room once and he had a big model train set lovingly laid out, which has always seemed somewhat incongruous to me.

Most of the times I ran into Pete, though, it usually involved taking drugs. I remember bumping into him at an AC/DC gig at Wembley Arena the following year. The two of us and a member of another quite famous rock band all ended up in a toilet cubicle snorting heroin. His other drug of choice at that point was Night Nurse. He spent a lot of time trying to persuade me to do cough medicine.

Pete had some crazy women follow him around on the road, too. There was this one particular girl, Audrey Hamilton, who turned up on several occasions. She was actually a very sweet girl, but damaged.

Not that sex was Pete's primary interest. He was a drug pig and would take literally anything.

You had to be very careful not to reap what you'd sown and I found that out to my cost with Audrey Hamilton. Audrey was one of the best-known girls on the scene, a beautiful Texan, but stark raving mad. The story is that Robert Plant wrote the song 'Hot Dog' on Zeppelin's last album, *In Through the Out Door*, about Audrey. Robert had escorted her for a time, but then could never get shot of her. Apparently, and simply to wind Robert up, Jimmy Page would pay to have Audrey flown out to Zeppelin shows all over America and then be sat right in the middle of the front row. Audrey also took a shine to me. That was no bad thing to begin with, since she was always the best-looking girl in the room. But if ever you gave Audrey more than a couple of drinks, she would cause the most appalling scene. She referred to members of our crew, and even Andy Parker as, 'Hey, asshole.' God, she drove me mad and was there for anything that was going. She would fly out to every show we did in Texas and then demand to be taken to me. Things got so bad with her, I eventually called up her husband and asked him to come and take her away. Yes, unbelievable as it may seem, Audrey was also married.

By the time we came off the road from that tour, I felt hollowed out from all the drugs, and the girls, and the seeming endlessness of it all. But also just as much from how strained relations were getting to be within the band. There was a feeling among us all that the band was getting stale, and I think Phil felt that the most acutely. He always said afterwards that we should have insisted on being able to take a break, and that it would have saved us. As it was, a certain amount of friction had developed between all of us, and there was lots more knocking of one another. Phil, though, was especially guilty in that respect and was having a bit of a spell of going off the rails. Not that I'm one to talk, but he would often be drunk all day and behaved pretty wretchedly at times. It had also begun to affect his performances. He'd forget his lyrics on stage and at his worst would sing crossword puzzle clues instead.

Ross Halfin: Besides Schenker going, I believe that another reason UFO weren't able to sustain their success in America was that Phil Mogg seemed to hold resentments against people. I liked hanging out with him, but he was a plonker at times and he appeared to get insanely jealous of other people. He didn't like this band, or that band, but I think that he was the one who behaved like a wanker. It was all a result of his own insecurities, which he covered up by drinking. And unfortunately, when Phil drank he turned into an even bigger dick. By the end of that tour of America, the rest of us would do our best to avoid him. The difference always was that Pete was a lot of fun to be around and especially to go drinking with.

Phil had also come to be obsessed about the music of Bruce Springsteen. I mean, his lyrics of that time were all sub-standard Springsteen rubbish: all this 'Joey rides the subway' kind of nonsense. That also took away from what had been so distinctive about UFO in the first place. Even their album covers got to be crap. They had done great album artwork with Hipgnosis; Lights Out *and* Obsession *were brilliant.* No Place to Run *and* The Wild, the Willing and the Innocent, *though, had shitty covers. And that pretty much sums up that period of the band. Everything about them by then had started to turn to shit.*

CHAPTER 9

*Satan and 'waffle dust' are co-joined and our hero takes
his own unique and ultimately doomed approach to
forging closer family ties.*

———

For all the tensions that had bubbled up to the surface, our next album was actually a relatively easy one for us to make. We did, though, record it in the idyllic setting of Queen's studio on the shores of Lake Geneva in Montreux, Switzerland. The problem was that *Mechanix* ended up a good way short of being our best record. As a band, we really needed time to recharge our batteries. Instead of which we were rushed back into the recording studio before we'd even properly worked up a new batch of songs in rehearsals. On more than a few occasions during those sessions, we would listen back to what we had cut the night before and realize that it sounded an utter mess. As we had arrived in Montreux short of original material, we decided to record a cover of Eddie Cochran's 'Something Else'. That's my biggest black mark against that album, since

133

it featured Neil Carter on his bloody saxophone. I hadn't even known Neil could play the sax until he overdubbed it on 'Lonely Heart', the first single we released from *The Wild, the Willing and the Innocent*. That song had turned out fine, but our version of 'Something Else' was hopeless. We made it sound more like Showaddywaddy than my old heroes, Blue Cheer. Even now, whenever I have the misfortune to hear that song, it's accompanied by terrible visions of overgrown berks in Teddy-Boy suits.

Our cause was also not particularly helped by our producer being such a larger-than-life character. A fellow Englishman, Gary Lyons had an undeniably great track record: he'd engineered all the classic Queen stuff with Roy Thomas Baker and also had success of his own with Foreigner. In our case, though, Gary's approach was not so much nose to the grindstone as to throw a party every day. He would want to take us out to lunch, even though we might only have started the session a half-hour earlier. Two hours later, we'd all of us reel back to the studio in a more than ever-so-slightly refreshed state. Not, it must be said, that we protested too much, if at all, about this relaxed regime.

One day, Gary even led us off on a wine-tasting excursion to the countryside. God knows how many bottles we sunk, but there was nothing of use recorded for the rest of that day. On the drive back to the studio, Gary was sat in the band's truck while we followed behind in a car. Not long into the journey, he climbed into the back of the truck, flung the rear doors open and began to hurl Andy's drumheads out at our car like Frisbees. Andy was fucking furious.

Poor Andy, though, was once again the butt of most things. When it came time for Andy to do his drum tracks, Gary set him up in the flat that adjoined the studio, supposedly to get a fuller sound. Gary also had a microphone and camera installed, so we were all able to monitor Andy at work. Each morning that Andy was due to record, Paul Chapman would pop down to the lakeside, buy a job lot of mussels from straight off a boat and then hide them in the little kitchen area of the flat. For the rest of the day, Gary would make Andy do take after take, and since it was the middle of summer and sweltering, the inevitable would always happen. We'd all watch with bated breath, pissing ourselves laughing, as Andy would end up almost sobbing into the camera: 'It stinks of fucking fish in here again!' I feel pretty sure that Roger Taylor never endured such indignities when recording in Montreux with Queen.

In spite of everything, *Mechanix* was actually our highest-charting studio album in the UK, a Top 10 hit. However, the British tour we did in support of it was blighted by the fact that Phil once again sang crossword puzzle clues. There was an especially disastrous gig we did at Birmingham Odeon where a guy in the audience also swiped the belt from Phil's trousers. Phil refused to go back out for an encore until the belt was returned to him, which upset quite a lot of the crowd that night. And it wasn't as if we hadn't had worse incidents of larceny happen to us. One guy once managed to get into our dressing room at Newcastle City Hall and tried to make off with a very rare Gibson violin bass stuck down the front of his trousers. He was only stopped by a vigilant security guard just as he was heading out of the stage door.

At one gig we'd be as good as ever, the next a bit of a shambles. Phil would sing the wrong words, or else end up on a different verse to the rest of us, so that we were never quite sure what he'd do next and the fans couldn't help but notice. I'd see groups of them on the front rows, mouthing along to a song, and then all of a sudden a look of utter confusion would cross their faces.

I think the problem was that Phil had just got bored with the grind of being in the band. In fact, all of us had grown disenchanted with things. I felt as if we'd begun to repeat ourselves musically, and that we were stuck in a rut. On the road, too, everything had come to be about how much booze and drugs we could get through each night. The rider in our dressing room was better stocked than a pub, with every kind of beer, wine, vodka and brandy you could wish for and bottles of Jack Daniel's. We went to ridiculous lengths to vary our booze intake, too. Phil and I watched a documentary about the singer Tom Jones on TV, in which Tom's doctor advised him to stick to champagne if he wanted to stay in shape. Each night after that, Phil and I would send the tour caterers out to stock our dressing room with two or three bottles of bubbly. By the end of the tour, the bill for champagne alone was ruinous. To be honest, I wasn't at my best on that tour either. For instance, I can't say that I didn't go on stage drunk, or otherwise impaired, on more than one occasion, which now I very much regret. In general, I was drinking heavily and then doing multiple lines of coke just to pep me up.

Pete Makowski: Of all Pete's vices, booze always was his biggest enemy. He'd often tell you that he'd stopped doing everything, while having a huge drink in his hand. I went out for a meal with him once and he kept excusing himself from the table. Eventually, I followed him and saw that he had a bottle of wine tucked around the corner. It's like he has to have his bit of naughtiness all the time.

Following the UK shows, we went out to mainland Europe as special guests to Ritchie Blackmore's Rainbow. I recall one particular show we did with them at a bullring in Madrid with Def Leppard opening the bill. The Leppard boys were big UFO fans and, at the time, still an upcoming band on just their second album, *High 'N' Dry*. Leppard's guitarist, Steve Clark, was a lovely lad, just twenty-two years old, but I remember him being very much worse for wear that night in Spain. Tragically, of course, Steve ended up pushing things too far and was dead within nine years. I know for a fact that the other guys in Leppard tried their best to calm Steve down, but for as long as you're still capable of performing, most other people who surround a band would be happy to let you carry on.

Leppard's singer, Joe Elliott, and I were near-neighbours and had by then grown quite close. Joe was a great bloke, but notoriously careful with his money. Back in those days, he'd never offer to chip in for the beers and a curry. And even when he became a multi-millionaire, Joe would turn up for a night out and claim to have no money on him, or else to have forgotten to bring along his credit card. You could also rely on Joe to empty the mini-bar in your hotel room and then bugger off without ever leaving a contribution to the bill.

A few years later, I was staying at a hotel in Hollywood and arranged to meet up with Joe. To give you an idea of how exclusive this place was, the actress Diane Keaton had the next-door room to mine. That night, Joe and I finished up being back in my room, me snorting up a mountain of coke, and him wiping out the mini-bar. Next morning, I was left facing a $2,000 bar bill and with Joe having fled the scene as usual. So I carefully counted up the empty bottles littered about my room, walked up Sunset Strip to a liquor store that sold miniatures, and restocked the mini-bar for a fraction of the price.

Joe Elliott: I'm sure Pete has said that I always forgot my credit card; wouldn't expect anything less. The truth is that I didn't have any money when the two of us first got together, and by 1984 when our Pyromania *album had taken off, he'd be round at my house emptying the bar. He is a pathological liar, but in the funniest sense. I've often told him as much. Ultimately, I'm a huge Pete Way fan, but like most people he's flawed and massively so.*

———

In America, we went out on a months-long arena tour with Ozzy Osbourne. Ozzy was just then riding high in the States with his second solo album, *Diary of a Madman*, and was trailed the whole tour by this religious nut protesting about his music. This mad bloke would turn up regular as clockwork at every hotel we stayed in, carrying a huge banner that read, 'Satan is here'. But then, if it wasn't members of the God squad, Ozzy always seemed able to outrage someone or other.

Ozzy had been one of my musical touchstones ever since I'd first heard Black Sabbath, but we didn't meet until after he'd left that great band and was making his first solo album, *Blizzard of Ozz*, in 1980. Our two bands were both rehearsing at Nomis Studios in Hammersmith. To me, Ozzy seemed every inch a rock star with his long, flowing hair and a wild glint in his eyes. He would invite me in to their room just to watch his young guitarist, Randy Rhoads, in action. Randy was a big fan of Michael Schenker's and also of UFO's, and Ozzy described him to me as his secret weapon. He was certainly a special musician and a sweetheart too, and Ozzy was transfixed by his playing. The two of us otherwise used to go down the pub together and became good friends. Funnily enough, Ozzy had a house up in Birmingham at that time that he always referred to as Atrocity Cottage. Sadly, I never made it up to Atrocity Cottage, but we'd seen each other on and off ever since then and I had visited the new place he'd bought in Stafford in the West Midlands. In fact, I nearly killed Sharon Osbourne – or Sharon Arden as she was then – driving her up there from London in my Jag. Sharon must have had nerves of steel to get into the car in the first place, because she knew that I'd had a drink or two. It was the middle of winter and about eleven at night. I was going pretty fast, but trying to be cautious at the same time when a lorry pulled out in front of us. I slammed the brakes on, but hit black ice and the car span right off the road. Fortunately, we hit a crash barrier, which stopped us from plunging down a steep embankment. Without so much as even blinking, Sharon said to me, 'Don't worry, we'll get you another Jag.' I didn't get another Jag as it happened, but was well paid for my trouble, and Sharon took charge after the crash. She got us a lift from the lorry driver to the next service station and then a taxi to the house, ringing ahead to tell Ozzy what had happened. When we finally arrived, though, Ozzy never even asked about the accident. He was fussing instead about several bottles of champagne which he'd bought for the occasion and left outside to chill in the snow. They were far more important to him than his wife-to-be and me having had a near-death experience.

Ozzy and Sharon would also come over to my place in Twickenham. Well, Sharon used to come into the house and leave Ozzy outside asleep in their Land Rover. One of the things little Charlotte grew to like the most was going out with me to wake Ozzy and fetch him in. Sharon was planning to have children at the time, so would sit and chat with Jo while Ozzy and I went off to the pub. Ozzy was good company, but also a man of wisdom. Like Lemmy, he would often give me advice about not doing this or that drug – talk about the pot calling the kettle black. And he was the same then as now, which is to say very open, pleasant, funny, but dangerous too. You never quite knew what Ozzy was going to do next or who he might upset.

It wasn't as if Ozzy went out of his way to annoy anyone, but he liked to have fun at other people's expense. Every day in Ozzy's company was an adventure and I was always numb enough to be able to handle whatever might happen next. And with regard to what Ozzy was capable of doing, there were no limitations whatsoever. On the one hand, the two of us would have very in-depth conversations with regard to our families and personal lives. On the other, he would turn to me conspiratorially and say, 'Pete, what we need is some waffle dust.' Waffle dust was how Ozzy referred to cocaine. He once told me that it had brought out virtually all of the fallings-out in Sabbath, though that hadn't dented his appetite. I think he saw me as a sort of kindred spirit, and we spent an awful lot of our time together boozing or else looking for waffle dust.

On tour, though, Sharon would rarely leave Ozzy's side and wouldn't allow him a drink from the minute he got up in the morning until after the show each night. And when she did let him out of her sight, she would often say to me: 'Look after him, keep an eye on him and don't let him do anything daft', because he would if given the chance. All through that tour, the two bands spent a lot of time in and out of each other's dressing rooms. Generally, we also stayed in the same hotels and spent our days off together. I enjoy a good wind-up and it was particularly easy to pull Randy Rhoads' leg, since he was so wide-eyed and gullible. Whenever his girlfriend was due to turn up on the tour, I'd let slip to Randy that the girl he'd spent the previous night with had been spotted in the hotel lobby and was on the lookout for him. Poor Randy fell for it every time, but I never thought of it as anything more than harmless fun.

The last time I saw Randy was immediately after the show we'd done in Knoxville, Tennessee, on 18 March 1982. We were walking out of the venue together and I pulled the girlfriend prank on him yet again. On this occasion, though, I told Randy that my old friend Audrey Hamilton, who had now sunk her claws into him, was bound for Florida for our next scheduled show. Since Randy's girlfriend was due to meet up with him in Orlando, I left him almost demented with worry.

I didn't find out about the terrible events of the following morning until we'd arrived in Orlando later the same day. As usual, I'd been up all night doing coke on our tour bus and happened to catch a news report on the TV. Ozzy and his entourage had set off for Florida a few hours after us. One of their bus drivers, a guy named Andrew Aycock, had been a commercial pilot and en route pulled over at an airfield in Leesburg, Florida. Ozzy was still asleep on his bus at the time, but Aycock hired a light aircraft and took Randy and Ozzy's make-up girl, Rachel Youngblood, up for a flight. Once in the air, Aycock decided to buzz Ozzy's bus, but clipped the roof with a wing of the plane and crashed, killing everyone on board.

Randy was just twenty-five. UFO had to step in and play the Orlando show in place of Ozzy. It was at the 60,000-capacity Tangerine Bowl, but there was nothing glorious about that night. Ozzy was also under severe pressure to complete the remaining tour dates, so we flew on to LA to wait while he auditioned for a new guitarist. Ever since then, it's preyed on my mind that I never got the chance to tell Randy that I'd been joking about Audrey. Worse still though, Randy's girlfriend turned up at our LA hotel just a couple of days later. I expected her to be overwhelmed with grief, but instead she didn't miss a beat and tried to remove my clothes right there in the lobby of the Sunset Marquis. That's groupies for you.

Less than two weeks after Randy had been killed, the tour started up once again in Bethlehem, Pennsylvania. Ozzy, of course, was in bits, but it was the same for him as it was for AC/DC after Bon Scott's untimely death: you had no choice but to deal with it, live with it, and get back out on the road.

***Garry Bushell, former* Sounds *journalist:** I encountered Pete in New York in April of 1982. UFO and Ozzy were doing a show on the second night I was in town and by then my jet lag was really kicking in. I remember being completely knackered, but Pete sat me next to a very attractive brunette woman at the gig. This turned out to be his wife, Josephine, and Pete had equipped her with a little phial of cocaine to help keep me awake, which I thought a very gentlemanly gesture.*

Up until then I'd been covering po-faced punk bands like the Gang of Four for Sounds, *so to go out on the road with UFO was like a breath of fresh air. In total, being around Pete and the band was funny, wild and a bit dangerous. Pete was the only person I've ever known Sharon Osbourne to ban from Ozzy's dressing room, because she said he was a bad influence. That's how deranged Pete would be on booze and drugs, and he was that level of crazy for pretty much all of the two or three days that I was with him in New York. On the morning of the show, I'd found Pete in the hotel bar having a large double of something or other for breakfast, and with a slice of lemon for vitamin C. Ozzy was headlining Madison Square Garden that night and while he was onstage, Pete snuck into his dressing room and made off with several bottles of red wine. The two of us then hot-footed it back to the hotel with this swag, abandoning poor Jo at the venue. She finally caught up with Pete in the hotel bar once again, by which time he was well and truly sozzled. It was like a scene from a* Carry On *film, with Jo man-handling Pete into the lift while at the same time belting seven bells out of him with her handbag. I also interviewed Ozzy on that trip, and he said to me, 'They call me a madman, but compared to Pete Way I'm out of my league.' Ozzy went on to tell me that he'd christened Pete 'Mister Medinite'. That was because the only way Pete could get to sleep at night was to drink five bottles of Vicks' Medinite cough syrup straight down.*

Our own situation got bleaker the longer the tour progressed. Even before Randy's death, we'd done a show with Ozzy in Texas, right on the Mexican border, where Phil and the crew had got into a huge bust-up. Phil had been drinking and picked a fight with one of the guys, and the rest of the crew had turned on him. The situation was eventually cooled down and we made it back to our hotel, only for Phil to jump off the balcony of his room and break his arm. After that incident, the touring party split into two camps, Phil's and everyone else, and that made for an ugly atmosphere in and around the band.

However, for me there was even worse to come. Right at the end of the tour, I was approached by a then-unknown glam-rock band from New York, Twisted Sister, with a view to producing their debut album for them. I leapt at the offer, as much for having something outside of the band to do, but it was to have disastrous personal consequences. On one of our increasingly precious days off, I flew from Cleveland to New York to meet with the guys in Twisted Sister and their manager. Naturally, I made sure to have a good load of cocaine on hand for the occasion and returned to Cleveland on the Red-eye, wired to the eyeballs. I was met by a wife who wanted to kill me.

Jo had come out from England with Charlotte to join me on the tour. Unfortunately for me, a group of girls who'd followed the band all over the States for years had also just then caught up with us in Cleveland. These girls were fans, nothing more, and while I was away in New York had offered to babysit for Jo. Being very enthusiastic, they also decided, entirely innocently, I'm sure, to show her a collection of Polaroid pictures they had amassed of us on tour. At a certain point, Jo happened across two particular photographs of me with different blonde girls on my arm. One of the blondes was Jo's sister's flatmate, the other *was* her sister.

I'd taken my sister-in-law's flatmate out on tour with me while Jo and I were still living in Kew. That alone would have been hard enough for me to explain away, but Jo's sister meant a whole other world of trouble. She was a model and would on occasion have work dates in New York. If UFO happened to be on the East Coast at the same time, I would invite her along to see our shows. She liked the rock-and-roll lifestyle, and if she did come to a show would then spend the night with me. The two of us didn't have an affair, not as such anyway. But very obviously it didn't look good, not least because I'd never told Jo I'd even seen her sister outside of the family. If your wife's at home with the baby, you just don't crack on that her younger sister's hanging out with you in America, do you? I'll leave it at that, because I know how much hurt the whole episode still causes in their family.

At all events, I got in from New York at 6 a.m. and found myself on the wrong end of a hell of a fury. Eventually, I had to walk out on Jo in full flow to go and do a breakfast radio show with the band, which didn't ease my stress levels. I wasn't reticent about cracking open a bottle of Jack Daniel's that morning, that's for sure. Needless to say, soon after that Jo filed for divorce and those two pictures ended up costing me a bunch of money and also my second family.

CHAPTER 10

Of matters legal, professional and a grotesque
act of public defecation.

———

My personal life was in ruins and UFO was also coming apart at the seams. Wilf Wright was the next casualty of the band's feuding. Rightly or wrongly, we'd started to think that we should have seen more money for the years of success and what started off as a whispering campaign was ended soon enough by Wilf being fired. We quickly replaced him with a guy called Carl Leighton Pope, who was our booking agent and well known to us. Carl promised us a fresh start, but by the time we'd finished the *Mechanix* tour I had resolved to leave the band and go off on my own. I was fed up after so many years of touring and not happy any more with the music we were making. We were like a worn-out, diluted version of the old band. I meant to do something that wasn't so reliant on having a hit single or, by then, on getting onto MTV. I also didn't want to turn into a hypocrite and moan all the time about other band members behind their backs. I don't want to point a finger at Phil in particular in that regard, but he appeared to me to be going through what some people would call a midlife crisis.

Ever since then, Phil and the others have claimed in interviews that I never told them of my intention to leave. That wasn't strictly true. In actual fact, I called up Carl and let him know that I wanted out. Carl, though, implored me not to say anything to anyone else just yet, because he was in the process of renegotiating the band's deal with Chrysalis. I suppose he didn't want news of my departure to have a negative effect on the size of the contract the band might be offered. So I kept quiet, and walked out of the band just as soon as that bit of business was resolved. UFO went on to make their next album, *Making Contact*, without me, but it sold poorly and they lost their brand-new deal with Chrysalis as a result.

In the short term, I had the plans for the Twisted Sister record to occupy my thoughts. I also got a second offer to produce a new album for a London punk band, the Cockney Rejects. It was the Rejects' fourth record and they wanted to move towards more of a hard-rock sound, which of course was fine by me. However, the title of the album, *The Wild Ones*, turned out to be all too apt, since the Rejects were like nothing so much as a gang of football hooligans.

When the four of them weren't drinking, they were fine – pussycats, really. But if anyone so much as looked at one or the other of them after they'd sunk a few beers, all hell would break loose. They would all want to start a fight, and the Rejects' idea of diplomacy was to hit first and ask questions later. I found being around them very testing. If we went to the pub together, there would be a lot of, 'Here, that geezer over there's a cunt', and, 'Oi, what the fuck is he staring at?' I could do no wrong in their eyes and we managed to make a decent-enough album, but I spent a ridiculous amount of time trying to stop them from smacking other people at a moment's notice.

After that stressful experience, I went straight on to make Twisted Sister's *Under the Blade* album, which was much less trying as the band were so respectful towards me. In a certain regard, I took my lead from Ron Nevison. To record the basic tracks with the band, I rented an old barn in Battle, near Hastings in the East Sussex countryside, and used a mobile truck because I wanted to capture a live sound. It was otherwise very much my own particular version of producing, which is to say that most of the time I was stood around with a beer yelling 'Louder!' or else, 'Quieter!'

For the overdubbing, we moved to west London and Bryan Ferry's studio in Olympia. It so happened that Ozzy and Sharon had just then moved into her dad, Don Arden's place in Wimbledon, down the road from where we were working. Ozzy was waiting to start work on his *Bark at the Moon* record so was at something of a loose end, which was always a particularly dangerous state for him to be in. By then, Sharon had also found out from Jo about what precisely I'd done to bring about the end of our marriage and was by all accounts disgusted with my behaviour. However, she didn't mind the thought of me occupying Ozzy and called one night to tell me he fancied a night out. 'You will keep an eye on him, won't you?' she added, as always.

When I told the guys in Twisted Sister that Ozzy was going to drop by, they were almost beside themselves with excitement. Their singer, Dee Snider, in particular couldn't believe that one of his heroes might want to hear his own band's music. Sure enough, Ozzy rolled up and Twisted Sister hurried off into the main studio room to play for him. The thing with Ozzy, though, is that he gets bored very easily. Dee and the boys must have seen Ozzy bouncing up and down in the control room and thought he was having the time of his life. In fact, he was restless and fidgeting, and every five minutes or so he'd turn to me and ask in desperation, 'How long's this going to take, Pete? Can't we go to the pub now?' You would have thought I was subjecting him to a form of torture.

Eventually, and just to shut him up, I took Ozzy out into the car park for a fag break. Before stepping outside, I also had a sniff of heroin, just to top myself up for the night. While the two of us were stood around together, I foolishly told Ozzy that the house that adjoined the studio was also Ferry's. He said, 'Is it?' furrowing his brow, and I could almost hear the cogs in his brain whirring. Without another word, Ozzy was off. He walked up to the front door of the house, pulled his pants down and deposited diarrhoea all over the 'Welcome' mat that was laid out on the doorstep. Calm as you like, he then pulled his pants up again and walked back over to me, his face expressionless. The smell, though, was so revolting that I instantly threw up. Ozzy stared at me, looking concerned now, and said: 'D'you know what, Pete, you should give that stuff up.' I tell you, it was a sure-fire way of bringing the recording session to an abrupt end, and off the two of us trooped to the nearest boozer.

It was around the same time that by chance I bumped into 'Fast' Eddie Clarke. Eddie was Motörhead's guitarist and we lived quite close to each other, but unlike with Lemmy, I'd never got to know him that well. Eddie told me that he'd left

Motörhead and in bad circumstances, as much as anything else I think because he and Lemmy were such different characters. When he found out I'd quit UFO, Eddie suggested we do something together. Indeed, he was so keen on the idea that he wanted us to start a band there and then.

Initially, the two of us began to rehearse together just for something to do. Eddie's a very good guitarist and we got on well, though he tended to get a bit aggressive with a drink inside him. One afternoon, Topper Headon called in at the rehearsal place we were using. Topper had not long left the Clash, so Eddie and I cornered him and asked him to drum with us. He was a great drummer, too, but at that time also a heroin addict, which was why he'd been kicked out of his band. Topper was off the scale from me doing a line or two. He'd written 'Rock the Casbah' for the Clash, and then gone and spent all of his royalties on smack. Topper eventually got clean, but sadly with the trouble he was going through at that point, wasn't able to stick at it with Eddie and me.

After we lost Topper, I found out that Jerry Shirley of Humble Pie fame was available. The Pie's *Rockin' the Fillmore* was one of my favourite-ever albums, but, like a lot of us back then, that whole band had got hammered with their record contract and Jerry was working in Dorset as a painter and decorator. Eddie and I went down to see him and persuaded him to get back behind his kit, which was when the idea of Fastway, the band, really began to take shape.

'Fast' Eddie Clarke: Pete and I weren't great friends beforehand and the idea of putting a band together was very much on the spur of the moment. I was living in Chiswick at the time and of a morning Pete

would drive round to my place in his Jag. Fucking hell, that car was a complete wreck. It was one of those old Inspector Morse-style Jags, but filthy and the windscreen wipers didn't work. Pete would also never have put any petrol in it, so most of the time it ran on nothing more than fumes.

Neither of us had any dough, though. Things had got nasty between Motörhead and me and I don't believe Pete had walked away from UFO with more than two pennies to rub together. To tell the truth, between us we didn't have so much as a pot to piss in. However, I knew a geezer who had a rehearsal space and talked him into letting us have a room on spec. That band was entirely put together on a wink and a promise. We said to everyone, 'Let us have it for free now and we'll pay you back later.' Blow me, the first day of rehearsals, I found out that all of my gear from Motörhead was locked up in the next-door room. My guitars, pedals, amps, even my guitar strap – they hadn't let me leave the band with a single thing. Next day, I persuaded Pete to break into the room with me and steal it all back. Pete was shitting himself, white as a sheet he was, but we got the job done. See, right from the start, it was like we were in this thing together.

We had a blast, too. Pete's a lovely fella and very quickly we got to be tight with each other. I couldn't get enough of playing with him – absolutely loved it. Topper Headon, bless him, had his own problems and was never going to last the course. Pete mentioned to me that Jerry Shirley might be available and now you were fucking talking. Rockin' the Fillmore *was a record Pete and I both loved, so we drove down to Dorset to see Jerry and what a trip that was. I must have persuaded Pete to put a fiver's worth of gas in the Jag that day, but it was pissing down. There was muggins here, the whole drive, hanging out of the passenger side window, having to wipe the windscreen clear with the sleeve of me coat. Pete couldn't see where he was going otherwise and wasn't the greatest driver at the best of times. And that car was so knackered he wasn't able to get it out of second gear, not even on the motorway.*

There was another morning that Pete turned up on my doorstep. He had a can of Special Brew lager in one hand, as usual, and a bag full of demo cassettes in the other. He was raving about this singer he'd heard, an Irish fella. Pete put the guy's tape on for me. He was singing a Zeppelin song and, fuck me, he sounded more like Robert Plant than old Planty himself. That was Dave King, and we arranged for him to fly over from Dublin.

Dave had enclosed a photo with his tape, but you couldn't see his face for hair. He walked through the arrivals gate at Heathrow and you could have knocked me over with a feather. What a fucking hooter he had on him. I turned to Pete and told him, 'You're going to have to fob him off, son – he's too ugly.' But could he fucking sing? And that was that, we had ourselves a great little band.

Jenny Stanley-Clarke, music PR: *It was actually Eddie, Pete and me who put Fastway together. I was also still working for Motörhead at the time, so it was rather awkward for me since Eddie had walked out and left them in the shit. He asked me for help, though, and so the three of us hooked up in a very clandestine way. We had to be desperately quick about things, too, because both of them were running out of money. Pete came across to me as very sweet, charming and incredibly good-looking. He and Eddie were complete opposites. Eddie had a sharp brain and tongue, whereas Pete was nice but rather naïve.*

With Dave King in place, Eddie was able to fix us up with a proper heavyweight management team, Steve Barnett and Stewart Young, who were also at the time looking after both

AC/DC and Foreigner. No sooner had Steve and Stewart come on board than we were offered a deal with CBS Records. CBS's main man in the UK, Muff Winwood, personally came down to see us in rehearsals and wanted to sign the band on the spot. At the same time, I'd also offered Chrysalis first bite at Fastway. Four or five days went by, though, and I heard nothing back so assumed they weren't interested. It was only when CBS put a really good offer on the table, and it was a breathtaking amount of money, that Chrysalis waded in and matched it.

Eddie and the management wanted to go with CBS because they had been first to the party. And it was at that point that Chrysalis informed me that I was still signed to them and that they wouldn't release me from the contract. Eddie actually went and stormed into their offices, and ended up having a shouting match with the Chrysalis boss, Chris Wright. That didn't turn out so well for me either. In fact, soon afterwards I got a court injunction from Chrysalis through my door which effectively stopped me from working.

This all came about at the very same time that I was going through my divorce with Jo, so I found it very difficult to concentrate on the Fastway situation. Added to that, Chrysalis didn't offer me any hope for a solution, nor to be honest did my new managers or CBS. No one even bothered to pick up the phone to tell me not to worry or panic, so I began to feel as if I were being cut adrift. My legal fees also meant that I had run out of cash.

The whole dispute went on for weeks. I'm liable to get depressed even at the best of times and so sank to an extremely low point. Finally, I called up Steve and Stewart and told them I'd decided that there was no option for me but to leave

153

the band. I was too embarrassed to talk to Eddie, but I think he subsequently got the wool pulled over his eyes in respect of what had gone on. At all events, it was years before I saw him again, though we were at least able to pick things up again as mates.

'Fast' Eddie Clarke: There was a lot of interest in the band. I guess we were sort of the first hard-rock super-group. Three times Chrysalis were supposed to come down to rehearsals and didn't show up. I was saying to Pete, 'What the fuck is wrong with these people?' Of course, it was only when CBS came along in the meantime that they started up all the crap about holding Pete to his contract. Straight off, I went over to their offices and I could be quite aggressive in those days. I walked right through reception, barged into the main man's office, and said to him, 'Listen, you cunt, what's all this about?'

We would have sorted it all out for Pete, no problem. Once my managers and lawyer had got on the case, even a fool could have been made to see that they were being unreasonable. But Pete panicked. Over and again I told him not to worry and that we would take care of it for him. But we rolled up to rehearsals one morning and Pete didn't show. I tried to get hold of him, but there was no answer. It was the same thing the next day and the one after, and that was the last we saw of Pete. He was just gone.

———

I ended up signing away my share of Fastway. I felt bad about leaving Eddie in the lurch, but of course, just the following year they went on to have a hit in the States with their first album. However, Lemmy was more upset about that fact than me. I ran into him not long afterwards and he said to me, 'I've got a bone to pick with you. Well done for helping to make that cunt Clarke a star.'

Ozzy had got to hear of what had gone down with Fastway and rang to ask me to go on tour with him. I think it was an act of kindness almost on his and Sharon's behalf. But then, Ozzy's bassist, Rudy Sarzo, had also just then left his band and Ozzy needed someone to step in quickly. Since no one from Fastway or the band's management intervened to discourage me, and being on the road got me away from the more mundane parts of life, I accepted Ozzy's invitation. True enough, he did also offer me an awful lot of money for the gig, £5,000 a week plus daily expenses and as much fun as you could possibly have.

I don't believe I was recruited on account of my skills as a musician, but more for the fact that Ozzy enjoyed my company. The arrangement suited Sharon, too. With her manager's head on, I'm sure she thought I could act as Ozzy's chaperone. Since Sharon had Ozzy under her thumb, I was also a good person for him to have around as cover. Ozzy would always be able to claim to her, 'But it wasn't me, Sharon, it was Pete.'

To this day, I'm asked more than anything if Ozzy is as wild as he has appeared. The answer to that question is an absolute yes, he is and he does not give a fuck. A perfect example of that occurred at what I suppose you could say was my job interview. Ozzy had a UK tour looming and right before it kicked off, he and Sharon invited me out to lunch at a very exclusive restaurant in Mayfair that they then patronized. Allow me to set the scene. Sat at the table opposite us were two well-to-do-looking businessmen, while at our table Ozzy was holding court in his own inimitable and very loud way. At a certain point, one of the businessmen leaned over, attracted Ozzy's attention and said to him: 'Excuse me, but really, would you mind toning your language down?'

My immediate thought was that Ozzy was bound to retort, but he didn't, or at least not right away. He simply sat back in his seat and perused the menu. This was unusual for him and it felt to me as though we had dodged a bullet. The two businessmen also returned to their lunch and Ozzy, Sharon and I passed the next couple of minutes in an uneventful silence. And then, still without having uttered a word, Ozzy stood up. He smoothed out the creases in his trousers and walked over to where the businessmen were sat, whereupon he climbed up onto their table, pulled his pants down once more and pissed all over their food. His two victims were outraged. One sat with his mouth hanging open, face beetroot-red, while the other dashed off to fetch the maître d'. Even before Ozzy was sat back down at our table, Sharon had got her chequebook out from her handbag and was writing out a cheque in an off-hand manner that indicated to me that she was more than used to such incidents.

Ozzy wasn't in the best of places at that time. He was still getting over Randy Rhoads' death and also I think having to deal with the demands of his ex-wife. Indeed, before the opening night of the UK tour, he went back up to Birmingham and had all of his hair shaved off. He came back looking like a skinhead, wild-eyed as well, which tells you well enough his state of mind. The opening night of the tour was in St Austell in Cornwall. All of us in the band and crew had been told by Sharon beforehand and in no uncertain terms that drugs would not be allowed on the road.

However, I happened to know that a guy on the crew was bound to have access to coke, since he had in the past worked for UFO. After that first show, Ozzy confided to me that he was on the hunt for waffle dust and I made the mistake of telling him about my contact.

Back at the hotel much later that night, Ozzy and I were the last two people left in the bar and he decided that the two of us should go and find my man. After some more nagging from Ozzy, I went off to reception to find out his room number. Up the pair of us then went to the room and knocked on the door. The instant it was opened, Ozzy sprang out from behind my back and barked out at this poor guy, 'Have you got any waffle dust, then? *Have you?*' The bloke almost passed out in shock. I mean, there he was faced with the prospect of being sacked by Sharon, but confronted by the very man whose show it was. Sure enough, he sorted the two of us out and Sharon never got to find out. Ozzy had a way like that of getting other people to do things for him.

A few days later, we were up in Leeds and staying at a big old hotel right in the city centre. We had a day off and so Ozzy wanted to go for a lunchtime drink. He had to ask permission from Sharon first and she delegated me to make sure he only had the one. Off we went down the road and found a working men's club. There were all these toothless old dears sat at the bar and Ozzy asked each of them in turn, 'Do you want a drink, darling?' Sure enough, one drink wasn't enough for Ozzy and he settled in instead for the afternoon. It was always the same story with him. No matter how much he'd put away, if you were ever to ask Ozzy if he wanted another drink, he would give the same reply: 'Is the Pope Catholic?' When the pair of us did finally start to stroll back up to the hotel, we were met by Sharon driving the other way in their Land Rover and with steam coming out of her ears. The two of us climbed in the car like naughty schoolchildren, Ozzy into the back seat because he in particular was in disgrace. Sharon accepted from me that I had been blameless, but wouldn't speak to Ozzy. We pulled up at traffic lights, at which point Ozzy flung the back door open and made a run for it down the road. Sharon screamed at me, 'Go and get him, Pete! Get him or he won't come back!' I gave chase through the city centre – God knows what the two of us must have looked like – caught up with Ozzy and managed to drag him back to the car, whereupon the two of them made up. That, though, was the pattern of things with Ozzy and Sharon and a volcanic eruption was never far from the surface.

The boys from Def Leppard came along to see the next night's show, and Ozzy and I spent a long time with them in the hotel bar. Sharon had gone off to bed and eventually the Leppard lads made their exit, too. That was Ozzy's cue to campaign yet again for us to procure waffle dust. The trouble was there was no one on duty at reception by that time and hundreds of rooms in the hotel. We were also on the lookout for a guy named John and whose surname was just as commonplace. That, though, was not enough to deter Ozzy. He led me up through several floors, knocking on every door that we passed and asking at each if there was a 'John' inside. And we never did find our quarry that night.

Joe Elliott: The solitary occasion I've taken heroin was because of Pete Way, albeit completely by accident. It was in Leeds and Pete was playing with Ozzy. We were in his hotel room and he was chopping out a line when there was a knock at the door. Unbeknown to me, Pete's immediate reaction was to sweep the heroin into the first thing that would make it disappear, which happened to be my vodka and tonic. I drank my drink and set off back down the M1 with my driver. The whole of that journey, I was throwing up out of the car window and then for the next six hours afterwards, and I had no idea why. It was only a couple of years later that Pete told me what he'd done that night. Thanks, pal. But that's classic Pete, really. He is like a living, breathing Carry On *film and he's only got worse over the years. Not that I'm convinced Pete's carnage has all been as a result of naïvety. I think Pete's wanted to live that kind of life, believing that people expect chaos from him. I mean to say, you can't be that fucked up all the time and not know. It'd be like winning the Lottery every week and thinking you were nothing more than lucky. And Pete's not stupid, even though he's often liked to play it that way.*

The problem for me was that I didn't really fit in with the other guys in Ozzy's band. Ozzy's new guitarist, Brad Gillis, and the drummer, Tommy Aldridge, were both Americans and in particular didn't like the fact that I travelled with Ozzy and Sharon on their bus, while they were dumped on a separate one. To be honest, I found dealing with the two of them a bit of an ordeal. It didn't help that we'd only been able to do a day's rehearsal together, because the other guys had flown straight in from the States. Pretty much the whole tour, I was worked up about getting my parts right and not making a mistake. The shows, though, seemed to go down well and Ozzy stuck to me like glue the whole time, as much as anything, I suspect, to get away from Sharon.

It was possible that I could have carried on with Ozzy's band, but I got an offer from Chrysalis to put together a band of my own instead. Also, Sharon had by then, I think, grown increasingly concerned about my abilities to keep Ozzy in check. It wasn't that she wasn't good to me, but I always seemed to be in the wrong place at the wrong time when it came to her. Mind you, I'm sure that she knew only too well that whenever you told Ozzy not to do something, he would be bound to do it.

Afterwards, I would hear second-hand stories about Ozzy's and Sharon's legendary bust-ups and they never failed to amuse me. There was one in particular about an argument between them in a hotel room, when Ozzy locked himself in the bathroom. Apparently, while he was holed up in there Ozzy decided to remove all the tiles from the walls. Sharon summoned the hotel manager, who eventually persuaded Ozzy to open the door. And there he was, surrounded by all these neatly piled-up tiles, like a demented Bob the Builder.

'Fast' Eddie Clarke: *Next thing I knew, Pete had popped up in Ozzy's band and Sharon-fucking-Osbourne had poached him from me. She had known Pete was in a right state over the business with Chrysalis and behaved like a total cunt. And then what happened? She and Ozzy went and shat all over Pete. He was supposed to do the whole world tour, but they kicked him into touch after just a handful of British shows. Apparently, Tommy Aldridge told them he wouldn't play with Pete. It was a crying shame, because Pete and I had a great thing going together, we really did, and I missed him.*

The trouble with Pete is that he's his own worst enemy. He never called me after walking out on Fastway, not even once out of courtesy.

I know that he's let other people down and suffered because of it, but he broke my heart. I get torn up from thinking about it even now. Four, five years later, I ran into him again on the road outside his house. It was good to see him after all that time and he invited me in for a cup of tea. I asked him: 'Now, what the fuck did you do that for, piss off without so much as a by your leave?' He couldn't give me an honest answer even then. That's Pete for you. We were good mates and he pulled a disappearing act like that on me.

PART THREE:

Crash

CHAPTER 11

*A new flight of fancy brings ghosts, Roman-style orgies and
a dead rabbit to the party, but our hero then crashes
back to earth with a resounding bump.*

———

The discussions with Chrysalis about my putting a new band together had actually started before I went out on tour with Ozzy. I had also retained the services of Steve Barnett and Stewart Young as my managers. That might seem odd given what I've said about how Fastway ended up for me, but from a purely business point of view I had every faith in the pair of them. As managers, they were tough, uncompromising, very thorough and in a position to get advances for both Fastway and my new band. So they were hardly going to be crying over my departure from Fastway. And after all that I had recently been through, I didn't want to be sat around waiting for something to happen.

As a result of Steve's and Stewart's negotiations, once I came off the Ozzy tour Chrysalis told me I could have *carte blanche* to form a band and offered me an amount of money equal to what Fastway had got from CBS. They also agreed to pay me a retainer, so out of my own pocket I was able to assemble the group quite quickly and pay everybody a decent wage. For obvious enough reasons, I think, I decided to call the band Waysted. What it boiled down to was that I wanted to make a grittier, harder kind of rock music than I had been doing with UFO and to get out there and play again.

To a certain degree it was like being thrown in at the deep end, so I sought out people I knew. The first person I got in touch with was Paul Raymond, who was available again, having left the Michael Schenker Group. I arranged for Paul to be flown over from his home in California and set him up in a nice house in London. I even took care to get him a nanny for his children. Just as he had been in UFO, Paul would once again be the key element of our band's sound, because he was such a solid rhythm guitarist. A decent drummer, Frank Noon, lived up the road from me and I soon got him on board as well. Frank had been the drummer in Def Leppard when they first started out. Indeed, he had recorded their debut EP with them, but decided to quit Leppard just before they made their first album. I'd imagine that has been a source of some regret for Frank ever since.

The first guitarist I thought of was an American guy I'd come to know, Ronnie Kayfield. Ronnie was a UFO fan and had been an eternal fixture on our guest-list whenever we had stopped off in his hometown of Philadelphia. He had told me often enough that he played guitar, so I flew him in too. Speed was also of the essence when it came to finding a singer and, in a roundabout way, I got to hear of Fin Muir through Ross Halfin's dad, Bob Halfin. Bob knew Fin's manager and passed

With Schenker's replacement, Paul 'Tonka' Chapman circa 1981: 'There was nothing that Paul wouldn't do to a ridiculous level.' *(above: © Pictorial Press Ltd/Alamy Stock Photo; below: © Andre Csillag/REX/Shutterstock)*

The Odd Couple, the author and Phil Mogg in mid-80s guise: 'Phil was the person who really kept a look out for me. Time and again he told me that he didn't want me to die.' (© Fin Costello/ Getty Images)

The deadly duo, Ozzy Osbourne and the author onstage and off. 'They call me a madman,' said Osbourne, 'but compared to Pete Way I'm out of my league.'
(above: © Tony Mottram; below: © George Chin/IconicPix)

The author and the Mad Axeman bury the hatchet, 1981. Says Schenker: 'Pete has had to endure such a long, deep dive into the valley of darkness.' *(© Ross Halfin)*

The author onstage with Twisted Sister and Lemmy at the Reading Festival, 1982. 'I recorded Twisted Sister's *Under the Blade* album. It was my own particular brand of producing, which is to say I was stood around with a beer yelling, "Louder!", or else, "Quieter!"' *(© Andre Csillag/REX/Shutterstock)*

Waysted at the Marquee and with guest Ozzy Osbourne at Hammersmith Odeon, October 1984. Osbourne, recalls the author, 'turned up carrying a dead rabbit that he had picked up from the butcher's that morning.' *(© Tony Mottram)*

With Waysted partner-in-crime Fin Muir and entirely superfluous teapot: 'At 7.55am precisely each morning, Fin and I would set off to get our first supplies of Special Brew and also several bottles of wine for the day.'
(Ray Palmer Archive/IconicPix)

Waysted's doomed 1986 line-up with singer Danny Vaughn (centre) and Chapman: 'A senior executive Capitol came along to the worst show of the lo in Detroit. He turne up late, too, so I had no chance to ply him with alcohol and drugs beforehand, and there was a cloud hanging over us from that momen on.' *(© Tony Mottram)*

The author circa his mid-90s dark days in Cleveland, Ohio. Recalls Def Leppard's Joe Elliott: 'Pete wanted the two of us to write a song, but he was too far gone to do anything.'
(© Mick Hutson/Getty images)

(*above*) UFO reunited in 1995: 'That was once again the top of a slippery slope.'
© *Mick Hutson / Getty images*

(*left*) Onstage with guest Slash at the Palace Theatre, LA on the 1995 reunion tour: 'Michael badgered me to read Slash the riot act. Slash said to me, "Wow, you of all people."' (© *Annamaria DiSanto / IconicPix*)

Still standing: 'The last and best thing I want is for this legend to get back out there and be just as good as he's supposed to be.' *(© Tony Mottram)*

his tape on to me. Fin's actual name was Ian and he was a typically forthright Scot. But the important thing for me was that he had a voice like a young Bob Seger, since I wanted someone who sounded very different to Phil. Fin looked the part, too, and wasn't entirely inexperienced, having sung in lots of pub bands. The two of us hit it off immediately, got on like a house on fire, in fact. I liked Fin for his bullish attitude, enthusiasm and also that he was able to help me write songs. I've always been able to knock together a few chords, but with Waysted I left the lyrics to Fin, just as I had with Phil in UFO.

The five of us began rehearsing at a small studio not far from my house in Twickenham. On occasions, Steve and Stewart, or else one or two people from Chrysalis, would pop down to check on our progress. They all seemed to believe in my vision for the band and like what we were doing. That being said, I didn't see myself so much as the guy in charge as being one of the boys. I guess, though, it fell to me and also to Fin to lead Waysted, and each of us took that side of things very seriously. However, we were equally committed to the fun aspects of being in a band. I've always believed the social side to be crucial for making good music. If the band gets on well together, that good feeling gets taken into the recording studio and up onto the stage.

To make our first album, *Vices*, I went back to the Hastings area, since it had been so beneficial for me with Twisted Sister. This time, we rented the ballroom of a quite grand old country hotel, Moor Hall, and again drove up in a mobile truck. According to local legend, Moor Hall was supposed to be haunted and it certainly had a chequered history. At one point in the more recent past, it had been bought by a very wealthy

Arab gentleman whose young daughter had then tragically drowned in a pond in the grounds.

In general, there was a very weird atmosphere about the place and we began to believe it was cursed. The pop singer, Paul Young, for example, was a guest at the same time as we were, and lost his voice not so long afterwards. There was also a particular room at Moor Hall that a number of guests had apparently asked to be moved from. One of the days we were there, a gentleman actually had a heart attack in that room. I was in the bar at the time and the hotel manager asked if I would go up and sit with this poor man and his wife until the ambulance arrived. I did manage to drag myself away from my beer, but unfortunately he died before he could be treated.

Another morning there, I woke up to find an elderly lady sat in the chair at the end of my bed. Next thing, she had vanished, and there were many other reports of similar strange sightings, so much so that they came to be almost run-of-the-mill. I'd always had a bit of an interest in the supernatural. As a teenager, I went on a Ouija board a couple of times. It was meant to be just for fun, but on each occasion the board spelt out things about Yvonne and me – where we would go on to work and that we would be married – and that freaked me out so much that I stopped. I've had a few other odd things happen to me, too. I was once sat next to a woman on a plane and no sooner had we got to talking than she let on that she was a white witch. She told me that I had three women who had looked over me ever since I was a small child. Since I'd lost my grandmother, great-grandmother and godmother when I was very young, it seemed to me that she had hit the nail square on the head.

For all the goings-on, we knuckled down to the album. I tried to keep it very live-sounding, just as I had with Twisted Sister, and we had some good songs, too. But to be honest my heart was still in Fastway, and looking back now I don't think I was able to give it my full attention. It also became apparent to me that Waysted was the worse for being a band that had been cobbled together rather than having evolved. Ronnie Kayfield, for instance, had never played to more than a couple of hundred people, and while he was able to overdub his parts in the studio, he was soon enough left cruelly exposed.

I, at least, had another distraction. I had met a beautiful young Danish model. Her name was Bethina and she was over in England on an assignment and lodging at the home of a photographer I knew. That English summer of 1983 was particularly lovely, as I recall, though that might have been the influence that Bethina had on me. I invited her out to Moor Hall for a day. Sure enough, she ended up staying the night and we were together for the next twelve years.

Bethina was just twenty-one, brunette and so striking-looking that she turned heads, but she was also a genuinely sweet person. No sooner had we finished our album than I followed her back out to Copenhagen and spent two weeks in the city shacked up with her and her mum. Bethina and I shared a sense of humour and she had a passion for travel, too, so over the years I took her out on the road with me a lot. It was then that I also discovered that she matched me in her appetite for booze and drugs, but that was never a cornerstone of our relationship. It was based instead on friendship and mutual company, and after a while even I grew to realize that these were things I couldn't live without.

169

Whenever she wasn't on tour with me, Bethina would return to Copenhagen, and so in the end I got us an apartment in the city and by the sea. In Copenhagen, the two of us had the perfect life together. The Danish winters could be grey and cold, but the city had great restaurants. In the summer, we would go to the beach. It was a great place for me to unwind and relax, and from then on we went back and forth between England and Copenhagen.

———

Waysted's *Vices* album came out in October 1983 but was met with no more than a muted reception. That was a blow to my confidence, but we had at least got a further chunk of money out of Chrysalis for tour support and I was more than happy to return to the road. To begin with, we went out as special guests on Dio's UK tour. In contrast to us, their debut record, *Holy Diver*, had been released to rave reviews and sold well, so we had our work cut out each night just to make an impression on their crowd.

I loved Ronnie Dio, though. Of course, he had one of the great rock voices, having sung on those classic early albums with Ritchie Blackmore's Rainbow, and even managed to fill Ozzy's shoes in Sabbath. After each show, our two bands would get together and Waysted wouldn't be able so much as to buy a drink, because Ronnie always insisted on picking up the bill. Dio's music was all a bit too dungeons and dragons for me, but whenever they played in London after that, I would meet up with Ronnie for dinner. He was a special, magical kind of person – loved to talk, which I liked – but was also very down to earth. There was nothing Ronnie enjoyed better than a pint of English beer and a curry. He wasn't particularly interested in cocaine or anything like that, but he took me at face value and as a friend, and his loss from cancer in 2010 was such a deeply sad one for me.

That version of Dio was by far the best, I think. Ronnie had the great Jimmy Bain on bass and a terrific young Irish guitar player, Vivian Campbell. Vivian was such an eye-catching performer that he couldn't help but highlight our weakness with Ronnie Kayfield. In big concert halls, Ronnie was out of his depth and, to be honest, he was at least part of the reason why Waysted initially failed to get off the ground. A lot had been expected of us, but we didn't hit it off as a live band, and on several occasions, Steve Barnett and Stewart Young told me that Ronnie Kayfield had to go. I stood up for Ronnie though, since it was me that had brought him into the band in the first place, and so it was eventually decided to recruit a second guitarist as backup. Unfortunately, I took another easy option and went for a guy Ronnie knew from Philadelphia, Barry Bennedetta, a decent player but again, no Vivian Campbell.

However, in the short term I was able to gloss over our issues as we were offered the opening slot on Ozzy's *Bark at the Moon* US tour. As always, Ozzy and Sharon were there for me and that tour was a red-hot ticket, especially since the three-band bill was completed by a cocksure young band out of Los Angeles, Mötley Crüe. The Crüe had just then broken into the American Top 10 with their second album, *Shout at the Devil*, and were establishing themselves as the new bad boys of rock.

In total, we did forty-five arena shows with Ozzy and the Crue. Each one was a sell-out, but since everyone was so desperate to see the Crue, let alone Ozzy, we were pretty much surplus to requirements. That tour, though, has since attained a somewhat legendary reputation that has more to do with what went on offstage. At the shows, it was actually a very smooth-running, professional set-up, but back at the hotel afterwards, well, that was another story and not one that really involved Ozzy. Sharon had ensured that between gigs he travelled on his own bus, as much as anything to keep him away from the Crue, so I didn't see that much of him. Perhaps not surprisingly, though, I did gravitate towards the Crue. Early on in the tour, their bassist, Nikki Sixx, told me that I was his hero and how he used to watch me do this and that, and would copy me. It was an odd feeling for me, being viewed as a kind of elder statesman and also to see Nikki get up to pretty much all of the things I had done in what seemed almost a lifetime ago with UFO. I really am talking about as many women, as much booze, drugs and general excess as one can possibly imagine. The Crue's guitarist, Mick Mars, was older and relatively more grounded than the others, but Nikki, their singer, Vince Neil, and drummer, Tommy Lee, acted as if they had just been released from handcuffs and years in captivity. It didn't matter which of their rooms you happened to stray into, the scene would be the same, and on every night of the tour. Each would be like a Roman orgy, naked women everywhere, and half-naked members of the Crue fucking them. On more than one occasion, Nikki called me into the bathroom and asked me to bring along his camera. He would be stood there, bold as brass, getting a blowjob and wanting me to take a Polaroid. There was also never a sense that any of the scores of girls that hung around the Crue were exclusive. We were all of us free to sample the goods and it was like picking out sweets in a shop. Nikki, Vince, Tommy and I also hung out over drugs. There was a ready, seemingly inexhaustible supply of coke in their dressing room, which they were equally happy to share. I grew to like them very much.

A funny thing was that, most nights, a shy, quiet young kid was also sat in a corner of the Crue's dressing room. He shared their manager, Doc McGhee, and would be off to one side while the Crue were having water pistol fights, snorting lines or else glugging on Jack Daniel's. He introduced himself to me one night as 'Jon', but I didn't think too much about it at the time. It wasn't until I bumped into him by chance two or three years later and he was bigger than God that I realized who he was. I was at the Marquee watching a Lita Ford show and got a tap on my shoulder. He was like, 'Hey, remember me, it's Jon, Jon Bon Jovi?'

Mind you, at that point anyone would have seemed shy next to the Crue. For me, though, the camaraderie that was had on that tour was what made it so special, because it had been a while since I'd experienced that and to such a degree. That's why I think Ozzy liked having people like the Crue and me around. He once told me how things had been hard for him when he first left Sabbath and that he'd had no option but to simply hire a band. I got the sense from him that he had no real, true friends. He had got to be a star, but that's not much fun if now and again you can't have a good blowout with your mates. I think Ozzy always missed being in Sabbath for that very reason.

The tour was so successful that a second leg of dates was quickly lined up, but unfortunately Chrysalis had concluded by then that they'd forked out more than enough on Waysted. Fin and I were basically told to go away and sort the band out. *Vices* hadn't sold and the label weren't interested in anyone but the two of us. I no longer had any particular qualms about getting rid of Ronnie, or indeed Barry or Frank. Paul Raymond, though, had been crucial to me, but he'd had a falling-out with Steve and Stewart, most likely over money, and spoken with his usual lack of diplomacy. They told me I had to fire Paul, and on this occasion I went along with them. That was why I was never able to be a leader as such. Too often, I accepted what was being said to me at the time and believed the best way to keep the show rolling was to keep my mouth shut.

As it happened, Fin and I tried out various musicians and recorded a batch of demos, but Chrysalis still weren't satisfied and decided not to pick up their option on the band. Strangely enough, it was at that precise point that Steve and Stewart also lost interest in me. I was back at square one, but determined to keep Waysted a going concern, and as luck would have it, just then UFO broke up. That meant, of course, that neither Paul Chapman nor Andy Parker had a job. Steve Harris had also offered me the support slot on Iron Maiden's up-and-coming *Powerslave* UK tour, so I asked Paul and Andy to come along and do it with Fin and me. At the same time, I happened across a good rhythm guitarist, Neil Shepard, and quick as a flash I'd got myself a tight little band, a sort of default UFO except for the fact that all of the songs were mine.

That also extended to our new manager. Steve Harris convinced Maiden's management team, Rod Smallwood and Andy Taylor, to take care of us. I got on well with Rod especially. He was a typically bluff Yorkshireman and I'd known him since Maiden's earliest days on the London pub circuit. Rod would come on in the costume of Maiden's band mascot, Eddie, and lollop about in a skull mask. Rod and Andy hit upon an idea to bring in Wilf Wright to be part of their stable and make him personally responsible for Waysted. It seemed a perfect arrangement to me, too. I'd remained in touch with Wilf, and having seen first-hand how he had guided UFO from clubs to arenas, would often call him for advice. In no time, Wilf had sorted us out a new record deal. Music for Nations was a smaller, independent UK label, but had a good track record, having unearthed both Metallica and Megadeth. The owner, Martin Hooker, pretty much offered us a blank cheque, which was possibly a grievous mistake on his part. In the end, I believe we may have drained him of all the money he'd made on Metallica. Martin and his business partner, Gem Howard, though, were both terrific guys. Their attitude to business was to go to lunch first and ask questions later, which suited me to a tee. It seemed to work for them, too. We cut a mini-album in summer 1984 and Martin managed to get it into the UK charts.

After that, I took the new line-up of the band up to Rockfield Studios in Wales to make our second full album, *The Good, the Bad, the Waysted*. Rockfield was a good environment. We lodged at a nice country house a short walk from the studio and the local pub, and the five of us got along famously. In its entirety that session was, if not exactly a party, certainly very relaxed. I'd always hit it off with Paul Chapman in particular and he was in great spirits at the time. Paul would be fine so long as he had money in his pocket and could be persuaded not to take it to the limit too often. And back then, I was still able to tell him no.

We came straight out of the studio and onto the Maiden tour, which was a joy for us to do. The new record was suited to being played live and Steve Harris went out of his way to look after us. God forbid if a member of Maiden's crew didn't also do a good job for Waysted. Steve would stand at the side of the stage and watch our set each night. We went down well with Maiden's British fans and never better than the night Ozzy joined us at Hammersmith Odeon.

Sharon was in hospital waiting to have their baby, so Ozzy was cut loose and turned up at the Odeon with Noddy Holder and Don Powell from Slade in tow. For reasons best known to Ozzy, he was also wearing a dress and a German Army helmet from the Second World War, and carrying a dead rabbit that he'd picked up from a butcher's that morning. Ozzy and I shared the same accountant, Colin Newman, who had an office in Soho. Ozzy had made an unannounced visit to the premises earlier that same day and stormed into a meeting that Colin was conducting, swinging the lifeless bunny around his head. Colin had gone bonkers because of all the blood that Ozzy had sprayed over his office walls.

Soon enough, Ozzy got comfortable in our dressing room. There were buckets of booze on hand and the waffle dust came out. In fact, Ozzy became so at ease that he demonstrated to the room that he hadn't any underwear on beneath his dress, a spectacle I would have preferred to avoid. At a certain point, Ozzy also announced that he meant to get up onstage with us and sing his best-known Sabbath anthem, 'Paranoid'. I hadn't planned on having Ozzy come out bare-arsed in a dress and with a Nazi helmet on, but reasoned that there would be no stopping him.

As it happened, we managed to get through four or five of our songs without interruption. I could see Ozzy, though, stood at the side of the stage, and he was raring to go. Fin duly announced him and the place went completely nuts. I've never seen a reaction like it; people were literally running in from the street and from that moment Ozzy took control of proceedings as if we were his own band. He went charging off around the stage, dress flapping dangerously high, shouting at us: 'Come on, let's go fucking crazy!'

Afterwards, Ozzy was hell-bent on going to a nearby wine bar. I climbed into his car with Noddy and Don, and lo and behold, Ozzy's driver went straight into the back of the car in front. It was just a nudge, but the driver got out and began a negotiation with the guy he'd hit. After a couple of minutes of animated chat, Ozzy intervened to try and bring things to an amicable conclusion. He had, at least, changed out of the dress by then, and he pulled a couple of hundred quid from his pocket to give to the guy, who was instantly placated. Next morning, I called Sharon's office to check that Ozzy had got home safe and sound, as that much was never assured. I expected Sharon's assistant to answer the phone, but instead it was a more familiar voice. 'Fucking hell, Pete,' Ozzy said to me, 'I'm a dead man.' Ozzy, it transpired, was supposed to have gone straight from our gig to the hospital to see Sharon. However, he had never made it that far. Rather, he had spent the night in the park opposite Colin Newman's house. Apparently, he'd handed over another fistful of money to a tramp in order to procure a park bench to sleep on. And that was a typical night out with the Prince of Darkness.

177

———

The trouble with Waysted was that I had to keep on remaking the band from scratch. After completing the Maiden tour, Andy had to leave us. His parents were both having health issues and he didn't want to be hundreds of miles from them. I could, of course, fully appreciate Andy's reasons for going, but Fin's departure felt more like a betrayal. We had been invited out to Israel to do a festival show, but Fin refused to go. He claimed that we weren't sufficiently rehearsed, which was nonsense, and so we ended up having a huge falling-out. Fin had actually gone off and hooked up with a young English guitarist, Lawrence Archer. The two of them subsequently auditioned for Sharon Osbourne, but I guess they weren't what she was looking for because nothing was ever heard of that project again.

Paul Chapman became my new right-hand man. He knew an American guy, Jimmy DiLella, a keyboard player, and Jimmy in turn had contacts with a singer, Danny Vaughn, and a drummer, Johnny Dee. I arranged for the three of them to fly over from the States and to do the show with us in Israel, which went well. In particular, Danny was an instant hit. He had one of those classic American rock voices, like Steve Perry of Journey, so brought a new feel to the band. Like most singers, though, Danny could be precious and would get annoyed at the tiniest thing, traits that Paul and I in particular seemed to bring out in him. In short, Danny liked to sulk and I got used to having to cheer him up.

Inspired by Danny's voice, Paul and I wrote a batch of new songs which sounded to me more accessible and radio-friendly. Things had worked out well for us with Music for Nations, but the Maiden shows had put us back in the spotlight to an extent and I wanted to get another major record deal to give us the best chance of reaching a wider audience. And on the strength of our new demos, Wilf secured us a very large advance from EMI in the UK and Capitol in America. The caveat was that Capitol, in particular, pushed us towards an even more commercial sound. They envisaged us crossing over to a mainstream audience, particularly in America, where so-called Hair Metal was then at its peak. This was an era in which bands like the Crue, Bon Jovi and Poison sold millions of records. If you went out to the States or watched MTV, you would see all of these guys with more make-up on than their girlfriends. Certain members of our band were more inclined towards that look than others, but to me it seemed ridiculous. I never had any desire to look like an advert for Max Factor. Rock and roll was in my blood and it was also quite a task for me to have to sit down and write a big, middle-of-the-road ballad like the Crue's 'Home Sweet Home' or Bon Jovi's 'Wanted Dead or Alive'. In the back of my mind, I worried that we would come across as opportunists, or a copy band. But then, I thought EMI's and Capitol's half-million was compensation enough.

There were other fringe benefits, too. We flew out to Ibiza to make our next album, *Save Your Prayers*. The studio was located in the middle of the island, away from the distractions of the main town, San Antonio, by day at least, and had a set-up like George Martin's in Montserrat with a pool right outside the door. Each evening, we'd have a barbecue in the grounds, after which we would retire to the clubs and bars of San Antonio, like holidaymakers. *Save Your Prayers* turned out to be exactly what the label wanted, slick and polished and certainly not as raw as I'd have liked. The songs were strong enough, but very precise and built to order. Nonetheless, the album never got any higher than 185 on the *Billboard* Hot 200 chart, so was hardly the crossover blockbuster that Capitol had been banking on. The plain fact was that Danny might have had a great voice, but our fans didn't want to hear a guy who sounded like Steve Perry on a Waysted record.

However, the killer blow for us with Capitol was that we took up a chance to do the East Coast and Midwest legs of Iron Maiden's North American tour. And at that point, it was absolutely the wrong bill for us to have been on. We'd have been much better suited to going out with the Crüe, or Poison, or even Def Leppard, and perhaps might have been able to find a new audience. As it was, next to Maiden that incarnation of Waysted came across as rock lightweights. Their American crowd were fierce partisans and we had a bumpy ride with them to say the least. Typically, a senior executive from Capitol came along to the worst show of the lot for us in Detroit. He turned up late, too, so I had no chance to ply him with alcohol and drugs beforehand, and there was a cloud hanging over us from that moment on.

Adding to my misery, there were internal problems with the band as well. Notably, Paul Chapman had once again begun to behave recklessly and started to demand money the band didn't have. In fact, our old label Chrysalis was still siphoning off my royalties from UFO to try to repair the damage that was done to them by Waysted. Eventually, Rod Smallwood and Andy Taylor intervened and suggested Paul sign on the dole instead, which is to say they sacked him. By then, I wasn't about to argue.

I tried to soldier on with the band. We brought in yet another guitarist and did some club dates of our own in LA, but Capitol went cold on us. To be fair to them, we'd done nothing to justify the amount of money they'd shelled out on the band. I flew back to England and spent the next year trying to pick up the pieces of Waysted. Soon after, though, Nirvana and the whole grunge thing happened, and the music business was changed at a stroke. Grunge sent all of those Hair Metal bands up shit creek without a paddle. Unfortunately, the idea of Waysted went right along with them.

CHAPTER 12

*An opportune encounter leads to the resurrection of the
old band with predictable results and ultimately
yet another tragic consequence.*

———

Once Waysted had finally fallen to ruin, I felt completely wrung out. Bethina and I had found a place to rent in Chiswick, just off a big traffic roundabout, and I spent days on end just staring at cars out of the front window or else at our own four walls. I am always liable to get myself into trouble when I have nothing to do, and sure enough began to booze heavily and take lots of sleeping pills. One afternoon, though, I managed to venture into town and, quite by chance, I bumped into Phil. Of course, we ended up in a pub. It wasn't as if we had been strangers to each other over the last four years or so; there'd been intermittent contact. Phil had endured his share of hard times, too. He'd gone through a divorce, like me, and had tried to hold UFO together and make records without me that the fans would accept, but it had been a struggle for him.

That day, though, it was just as if the two of us had picked up where we'd left off after making *Obsession*, and within a couple of hours we'd started to discuss the possibility of working together again.

After years of slog and frustration, it was such a relief for me just to talk to Phil. He'd moved up to Birmingham in the interim, and as we parted, he invited me up there. On reflection now, Phil might well have intended the offer to be just for a weekend. But within a matter of days, I had driven up to Birmingham unannounced, knocked on his front door and moved in with him. I ended up staying with Phil for two or three months, but in that time we wrote a bunch of songs together. That aside, like a couple of old men we slipped into a thoroughly ridiculous routine. Every morning, the two of us would walk to the video store up the road, rent out three, four or even five films, and then crash out that night watching them. The problem was that neither of us could remember which film we'd seen from one night to the next. Often as not, we'd be sat in front of the telly of an evening and one of us would turn to the other and say, 'Here, I'm sure we saw this one two days ago.' It was amusing at the time, but also a good indication of just how much I at least was drinking by then. The thing was, I'd cut back on coke and heroin but used alcohol to fill the vacuum. I'd also convinced myself that it was best for me to work in a somewhat altered state. You see, you can't automatically write a great song, but if I'd had a few drinks I seemed better able to come up with chord patterns and hum melodies. Drunk, I could write a complete song in minutes. It was as if my best ideas came to me when I wasn't capable of thinking too much.

183

Since things had gone so well musically with Phil, I decided to buy a house in Birmingham for Bethina and me. I found one within walking distance of Phil's, at Rathbone Place in the Harborne area of the city. Bethina moved up and soon after we got married, at West Bromwich registry office of all places. By then, I think Bethina's family kind of expected it of me. And since I'd been married twice before, Bethina had also started to ask, 'Why not me?' Mum, Dad, my brother Neill and his wife came up for the ceremony, Phil was best man, and for as long as it lasted it was a very happy marriage.

Neill Way: Mum and Dad did worry a lot about Pete, even as an adult. Mum in particular would get very upset if she read about his drinking or drug taking. The thing was, though, no matter what you might say to him about it, Pete would never listen. I think he believed he was indestructible. There were also protracted periods when he wasn't that communicative with the family, so it always fell to me to sort things out for Mum and Dad whenever they had problems. Yet irrespective of what Pete did, or however long he might have left it without getting in touch with them, they would always welcome him back with open arms. And no sooner would Pete come back into our lives than he would disappear from them again.

It seems unfeasible to me now, but in total it took three or four years for Phil and I truly to get back on our feet again. There were bumps along the road, too. Once we had enough songs for a record, we started to look for a guitarist and drummer. I remembered Laurence Archer from the work he'd done with Fin, and didn't bear him any grudge. More important than that, Laurence was a talented musician and as luck would have it, had also been playing with a very able drummer, Clive Edwards, who'd previously worked with Pat Travers and Jimmy Bain's Wild Horses. The four of us began to rehearse together and eventually Phil and I determined that this could be a new version of UFO. My problem was that when we weren't rehearsing I found that I had time on my hands and so drank even more. Eventually, it reached the point where I had to admit that I was a full-blown alcoholic. I'd got myself into a pretty wretched state. I would be drunk from first thing in the morning, even at rehearsals so that I was incapable of contributing anything worthwhile to the band. In the main, I drank can after can of Special Brew, which wasn't pretty. On top of that, I could also get through a couple of bottles of sparkling wine a day. If you've ever seen those old public information films warning of the dangers of booze, they would have these helpless old geezers in them who couldn't even face the day without a drink. Well, that was me. At first light, I would walk to the newsagent's around the corner from me. I knew that it would be open at 6.30 a.m. for the papers, so I'd pick up a six-pack there and start my day off.

Since I was almost hopeless, Phil took it upon himself to find us a new manager, a guy named Robin Greatrex. Robin, in turn, had started to shop for a record deal for us. It was, though, like we were a new band again and took time. And the longer it took, the worse I got. Finally, Robin was forced to intervene and made all the arrangements for me to go into a rehab clinic in London. I didn't have much choice in the matter, but it was at least quite an exclusive place, housed in an old church and in a leafy part of the city. My fellow patients were bankers, lawyers and captains of industry, and quite a few celebs, too. Some of these people had lost their jobs and families because of alcohol. One guy, in particular, had ended up on the street and sleeping rough. In comparison to them, I started to think that perhaps my problem wasn't so great after all.

There were amusing aspects to being in there as well. Each morning, a fleet of chauffeur-driven cars would pick up or drop off people at the clinic. It was like attending a surreal sort of VIP bash, and a dry one to boot. Group meetings were held in a community room and we'd all be sat around on plastic chairs. The staff would ask if anyone wanted to share with the group. Some people took to that more easily than others. There was one guy who was a heroin addict and couldn't wait to chip in with another story about how he'd had to sell all of his possessions to buy drugs. It was supposed to be a support group, but whenever he volunteered to speak there would be lots of deep sighing and eye rolling. And no, I didn't bloody well share with the group. I used to hide behind someone else or stare at the floor. And I would never make the mistake of being sat on the front row.

In all, I spent a couple of weeks there and was put on what's called a twelve-step programme to recovery. I tried to stick to it and managed nine months without a drink. Being sober for that length of time felt to me like quite an achievement and physically I noticed the benefits, but I couldn't keep it up and eventually hit the bottle again. Quite simply, I was bored and just felt so much more comfortable within myself when I'd had a drink. To this day, I'd prefer not to drink as much as I do, but it still seems to me better than the alternative.

Funnily, now that I was in my thirties I also rediscovered my passion for running. I started to go out for a run every day and in all weathers. It wasn't as if I was impaired by the booze. I'd drunk for so long and imbibed so much that I would never wake up with a hangover. Even that addiction to exercise, though, did me no good in the end. I ran so much that I knackered my knees and was forced to stop.

We did eventually get a record deal, but only on the strength of the UFO name. So in the spring of 1991, the four of us retired to the compact Cornish town of Launceston to make what would be the band's fourteenth studio album, *High Stakes & Dangerous Men*. It was a happy time. Laurence was a great guitarist, Phil was singing really well again, and between us we eased back into the classic UFO sound. Indeed, to this day I'm still fond of that record. It was released early the next year and we toured the UK, Europe and Japan, but never made it out to America with that line-up. Good as the shows and Laurence and Clive were, Phil and I kept on having to deflect questions about Andy Parker, Paul Raymond, and most especially Michael Schenker. It also became apparent that it was going to be difficult for us to secure further investment in the current band, since the demand for it just wasn't great enough. Tough as it was on Laurence and Clive, people wanted the UFO of *Strangers in the Night*; it was that simple.

Michael had evidently reached the same sort of impasse in his career, because he chose that moment to get back in touch with us. He'd been in contact with a record label owner in Japan, a guy named Toru Hashimoto, who was prepared to put up an extremely large sum of money for Michael, Paul, Andy, Phil and I to reunite. It was again in the half-million-pound bracket for an album and tour, and at that point we were of course all receptive to the idea, at least in principle. Even so, the negotiations dragged on for the better part of two years before everything was sorted out, and mostly to Michael's satisfaction.

Once everything was at last agreed, the five of us regrouped in California to rehearse and write *Walk on Water*, our first new album together in seventeen years. A lot of water had indeed gone under the bridge and we set to the task at hand in an almost affable, but very business-like atmosphere. Everybody made a conscious effort to make the sessions productive and Michael in particular was on top form, though fussy about every detail, as always. In that sense, it was like we'd never been apart, though relations between us were much less fractious than they had been the last time we were in LA as a group, mixing *Strangers in the Night*.

Dare I even say it, but we acted like professionals. Rehearsals would begin at 11 a.m. prompt and we would work through till six or seven at night. The only drawback was that we were also battling against the clock. Since the label wanted to rush the album out for us to tour, we were only able to allocate the bare minimum of time for what is the crucial pre-production process. Time enough for us to knock into shape an album's worth of songs, but not one that would be able to stand comparison with *Lights Out* or *Obsession*. To be truthful, though, that would have been a stretch in any circumstance.

However, there was one man who could at least make it sound just as good as those two albums and that, of course, was our old friend Ron Nevison. So it was that towards the end of 1994, we also got back with Ron at Rumbo Studios in LA, where Guns N' Roses had cut *Appetite for Destruction*. Ron's manner hadn't softened in the intervening years and he still ranted and raved, a heart attack waiting to happen. But Ron's extravagant lifestyle had by then cost him his two Rollers and the mansion in Bel-Air, so his circumstances were somewhat reduced. During those sessions, he spent an awful lot of time in the bathroom. We began to put a stopwatch on his toilet breaks and on one memorable occasion he was in there for thirty minutes.

Prior to the actual start of recording, the five of us had made a pact not to drink for as long as it took to make the album. Alcohol, we all agreed, had been one of the biggest causes of our past downfalls. In the event, some of us stuck to that less rigidly than others, though I tried my best to restrict myself to just a couple of glasses of wine with dinner. There was, though, one unfortunate occasion when I had to overdub a simple bass part for Ron. All I had to do was hit a single note, and Ron wanted me to come in on his count of four. It hardly sounds a test, but being stone-cold sober, I just wasn't able to do it. After twenty failed takes, Ron turned scarlet and screamed at me, 'What is it, have you lost your fucking ability to count to four?' His hairdryer treatment would always reduce me to a quivering wreck, so I confessed to him that I could murder a drink. He was quite relieved, I think, to send me off to get one. When I returned to the studio, I was finally able to play the part. That, though, was once again the top of the slippery slope. Not long afterwards, Bethina flew out from England to be with me and I took her with me to pay my old friend Rick, the drug dealer, a welcome visit.

Michael Schenker: From the time UFO got back together in 1994, Pete seemed to me to change an awful lot. It was as though the life force slowly drained out of him. The Walk on Water *record was actually a*

189

positive start for us all to reconnect and Pete was OK in that period, but as time went on he started to look and behave very weirdly.

———

Walk on Water turned out to be a decent enough record, but didn't sell as well in America as we'd anticipated. Nevertheless, the US tour we did behind it was a great success, in terms of ticket sales at least. Andy, though, didn't join us on the road, which somewhat undermined the whole exercise for me. Always his own man, he decided instead to return to England and take over the running of his Dad's manufacturing business with his two brothers. He had also not long remarried and I think his new wife was reluctant to let him clear off on tour with us. As I'm living proof, touring can be an exciting adventure but not necessarily for wives.

At all events, people flocked to the shows, if only just to see Phil, Michael, Paul and I stood together on stage. It didn't seem to matter whether our performances were good, bad or indifferent. In that respect, we had graduated to becoming a classic rock band. I'm not sure, though, that there was the same communal spirit in the ranks. In the first instance, that had come about from us having to fight together to get a reaction from audiences; now we could've all gone on and broken wind and got an encore.

In Andy's stead we brought in another fine drummer, Simon Wright. Simon had done a stint with AC/DC, which was a big tick in his favour for me. He was great company, too, but Michael thought he played too loudly and was forever complaining about this. I knew from bitter experience when to be seen and not heard around Michael onstage, but Simon was a powerhouse on the kit and hit his drums very hard. It became routine for us to bring the house down. And if ever an audience was slightly subdued, or the band off-colour, we could always pull out an ace from up our sleeve like 'Too Hot to Handle' or especially 'Doctor Doctor'. Those songs seemed to have taken on a life of their own. They were a major part of our legacy, but over the years had grown bigger and more universal than us. It was a different matter, though, whenever we tried out the new material. People clearly hadn't come along to hear the latest record, which I suppose is the fate of every band.

Every show, just about, we sold out. We even broke the house record at the House of Blues in Chicago; a six-night stand and all the tickets went in just two days. In LA, we played the Palace Theatre on our old stomping ground of Sunset Strip. Slash got up that night and performed 'C'mon Everybody' with us. He turned up at 5 p.m. prompt for sound-check, meaning to go home to his wife and then return for the show. Michael, though, badgered me all afternoon to read Slash the riot act before he left. Apparently, Michael had seen Slash jam once before when he hadn't been in the best of states, and he was fixated on making sure that didn't happen to us.

Slash seemed to me totally focused, but I did eventually pull him to one side. I said to him, rather awkwardly, 'I hope you don't mind, but Michael has asked' − I had to throw that in − 'could you not be fucked up when you come back?' Slash peered at me from under the brim of his top hat and said, 'You don't remember the first time we met, do you?' And I couldn't specifically. He went on, 'Well, you were *so* fucking wired at the time. So I can't believe what you've just said to me.

191

I mean, wow, you of all people.' I was like, 'Well, OK then, see you later.'

That aside, the tour ran without a hitch for a couple of months and then hit the buffers on 22 October 1995. The catalyst was a misunderstanding between Michael and the rest of us. Michael was travelling separately in a Winnebago with his then-partner and so-called personal assistant, the late Bella Piper. We had done a show in Redondo Beach, California, on 21 October and were due to play the next night upstate in Modesto. Bella, though, misread the tour schedule and mistakenly thought we had the following day off. In the event, the rest of us were at the venue in Modesto and waiting to go on stage when we got a frantic call from Michael to tell us he was en route. However, he was not due to arrive until going on midnight and since the audience was already growing restless, we had no option but to cancel the gig. That news, of course, went down like a lead balloon and people started to pelt the stage with missiles. The road crew had to go out and rescue our gear, and told us it was like stepping in front of a shooting gallery.

When Michael did finally turn up there was an almighty bust-up between us and him, which ended with the band going its separate ways once again. Michael, to be fair, did try to apologize on this occasion, but Phil in particular was having none of it. That also left me with a very difficult decision to make, and one I'd envisaged being able to postpone for a good few weeks yet.

At an earlier show we'd played in Columbus, Ohio, I had met the woman who would go on to be my fourth wife. Her name was Joanna Demas and she was a doctor. In actual fact, Joanna had the distinction of being the first doctor to pose for

Playboy magazine, which had caused quite a stir at the time. A friend of mine, Brian Wheat, who played in the band Tesla, had inadvertently brought us together. Brian had consulted Joanna for treatment and the two of them had remained in touch. Joanna was a big rock music fan and Brian had called her to tell her that his mate's band was coming to town, and then asked me to put her on our guest-list for the show.

Joanna was more than ten years younger than me, but we appeared to have a lot in common and that night hit it off like old friends. I made plans to see her again when the tour ended, which I anticipated would allow me the time to think of an excuse to give Bethina for my delayed return. My marriage, I'm sad to say, had by then followed an all-too-familiar path. Bethina had got fed up with me going away all the time. Rather than follow me around on tour, she came to prefer going back to our apartment and her family in Copenhagen. It wasn't as though we had separated or fallen out, but a distance had grown between us and the demands of my lifestyle were pulling us ever further apart.

Ultimately, I just wasn't able to settle down for long periods and I loved being on the road too much to give it up. I also craved new experiences, and in that sense Joanna, right then, was like a beacon to me. Shamefully, though, I didn't even try to resolve my differences with Bethina. Instead, rather like a child who can't face confronting a parent, I simply called her up, told her I wouldn't be coming home, and then flew directly to Columbus and moved in with Joanna.

At the time, I never stopped to consider the effect of my actions. It was easier for me not to look back, to press ahead, as if I were doing nothing more than going from one gig to the next. I could never, though, entirely outrun my past. I did see Bethina on and off over the years, but by then she was also drinking heavily and taking too many drugs, prescribed and otherwise. The two of us used to drink and do plenty of coke together, but casually, and I'd never sensed during our marriage that she had a deeper problem. After we parted, though, I found out that she had begun to develop problems with her liver. I tried to get her to cut out the booze and pills binges, but she wouldn't listen or else was past the point of caring. She would tell me how she'd just get so bored if she didn't drink, which I at least could appreciate.

Over the next few years, Bethina was in and out of hospital. She was under doctor's orders not to drink, but didn't have it in her, or want to stop. We actually had a night out together when I had a show to do in Copenhagen in the spring of 2007. By the time she arrived at my hotel that evening, she'd already had two bottles of wine. I took her out to a nice restaurant, but I don't think either of us ate even a crumb. It was instead a liquid meal and that was the last time I saw her alive. The next time, she was in her coffin. It wasn't long after that night that I got a call from Bethina's brother. He told me that her liver and kidneys had failed and that her doctor had informed the family that she wouldn't pull through. I flew straight out to Copenhagen, but didn't get there in time. Bethina had died in the hospital earlier that evening. Of course, I've thought since about whether Bethina could have died of a broken heart, but I don't believe, or perhaps can't accept, that to be true. What happened to her was desperately sad, but I'm sure there was nothing I could have done to stop her from effectively killing herself. The one thing it is possible to say is that since Bethina had spent so much time living with me, she would've known just how hard it is to say no to certain drugs. By the time of her death, I had also begun to consider a possibility that now seemed very real to me. That I was somehow dangerous to other people, or if not that, then cursed.

CHAPTER 13

*In which an inventive use is found for a birthday cake
and the trials and tribulations of shooting up on a
commercial airline are laid bare.*

———

Joanna's house had been built around the time of the American Civil War and was near enough a mansion. It had three floors, a ballroom on the second, servants' quarters on the third and God knows how many bedrooms. She had trained as a junior doctor in her native Miami and then moved to Columbus to establish her own practice, which was based at the city hospital, where she also interned. She specialized in laser surgery, but also did liposuction and Botox procedures, as well as the more general medical stuff. I was devoted to Joanna and wanted to spend every second of the day with her. So much so that I would go into the office with her every morning and even help out with the filing or answering the phones. In turn, Joanna was more than enthusiastic about my music and loved creative people. If ever I had a breakdown because of my drinking or I was using, she would simply tell me, 'That's OK, you're an artist.' In that respect, I lived up to what Joanna wanted me to be, but we also became great friends and ours was a whirlwind romance. I got a divorce from Bethina and, eight months almost to the day after I had moved in with Joanna, the two of us were married. It was my fourth go at marriage, and Joanna's second. Her first husband was a fellow physician and had trained with her in Miami, but they had separated soon after moving to Columbus together. In a way, Joanna had a very old-fashioned idea of marriage. She expected a husband to support her, so it was me who paid the mortgage on the house. She would buy me presents, clothes mostly, but we split everything else 50-50. Soon enough, that included our drugs.

It was only after I married Joanna that I started to use needles. To begin with, we had confined our consumption to booze and unlimited amounts of pills. One of the great advantages of living with a doctor was that she was able to write out a prescription. Like I said, I enjoyed going into work with Joanna, but her twenty-second-floor office at the hospital was also where the drugs were kept. Every time I visited, I would make a point of checking out what she had in her medicine cabinet. One day, I found a bottle of liquid morphine in there and, being the great adventurer, decided on the spot to give it a try. And obviously, liquid morphine had to be injected, so I gave myself a shot.

The catalyst for Joanna's and my drug use escalating was a neighbour of ours dying from AIDS. As part of Joanna's intern duties at the hospital, he'd been a long-term patient of hers as well as a friend. In the latter stages of his illness, Joanna would

197

ask me to go in and see him, to try and lighten his mood, which I was able to do to a point with gallows humour. On one such occasion, I said to him, 'Look, if you are sure that you're going to go, can you leave me your supply of morphine?' Later, though, he begged Joanna to overdose him, said he wanted to be let go, though as a doctor of course she declined.

Joanna was devastated when he did at last die. She cleared out his room and brought all of his morphine back home with her, intending I'm sure to get rid of it. However, that night she told me that she felt like doing a shot, and asked me to join her. There was so much of the stuff that we did some more, and then more again. The following evening, Joanna came home and said to me, quite calmly, 'Could we get some heroin?' From then on, it was as though each of us encouraged the other to plunge deeper into addiction.

Straight away, Joanna would mainline her heroin, which is to say shoot it into her veins. Initially, I preferred to take it like a shot from the doctor, up my bum. It wasn't too long, though, before I came to understand that you would feel the effects of the drug even more by going into a vein. If you mainline heroin, the reaction you get to it is so much faster and more intense. It was, I believed, the ultimate euphoria, but the trouble was it didn't last that long.

That's the trap of heroin. The more of it you take, the more you need to do. It *is* exactly like Guns N' Roses said in that song of theirs 'Mr Brownstone': 'I used to do a little but a little wouldn't do it, so a little got more and more.' Quite often back then, I actually preferred to inject from a bottle of morphine, rather than going through the whole procedure of cooking up heroin on a spoon. I told myself I wouldn't be tempted to fall for the lure of that particular ritual. And I was then sufficiently in command of my using to be able to maintain what you might call a public persona. That is, other people wouldn't have known I was on smack.

Soon enough, I had also sorted out regular supply lines for Joanna and me. Through Joanna, I got to know a guy named Gary Lee, who became a close friend. When Gary was still a teenager, his banker father had been killed in a car crash and had left him millions in a trust fund, so Gary had never had to work. He had, though, become a heroin addict and, as such, was eventually legally forbidden direct access to his estate – his mother administered it for him instead. Gary would have to ask his mum whenever he wanted to withdraw money. He'd tell her it was to buy guitars, and then sell them for smack. Gary was a former patient of Joanna's and the two of them happened to run back into each other one day. He wanted to get hold of methadone for his withdrawals and Joanna suggested he come and see me. The first time that Gary and I ever met, we shot up together in my kitchen. I'd never even spoken to the guy before then.

Gary had a contact in New York, and he started to drive to the city to score China White from him for Joanna and me. I also had another, let's call him friend, in LA who used to send FedEx packages to us. Each of these boxes would have a birthday cake inside. My friend would hide little lumps of Mexican brown heroin in the cakes and even enclose a birthday card. It was an inventive operation if nothing else. Soon, we were spending around a thousand dollars a week on smack. To start with, we weren't using cocaine, but then Demerol and morphine also became more regular parts of our diet and

I found that coke complemented each of them. So then we began to buy a thousand dollars' worth of cocaine at a pop as well. That amount would get you a lot of coke, and I could pretty much guarantee it would be uncut, so it worked out as being good value for money.

If you're using coke by itself you get a concentrated high, but opiates just kind of mellow you out. And once I'd had my shot, I could go about my business as normal – going to the shops, out to a restaurant, that kind of thing. I read once about a system that was pioneered in Switzerland, I believe. As long as junkies got a job and reported for work, then the state would supply them with heroin and morphine. They would have their shot for the day and go off into the office or factory, and then get their top-up dose in the evening. It was similar for me. So long as I got my fix, I was perfectly able to function, or at least I was in the very beginning.

Gary Lee: I sure did do the New York run to get heroin for Pete and Joanna. There was no good option in Columbus at that time and I'd lived in New York, so was able to take care of it for them. Up till then, Pete had been getting their stuff from a guy on the West Coast. I found out how much Pete was being charged and knew this guy was ripping him off. He was paying at least double the amount he should have been. That was a recurring theme. There was this other guy in Columbus, Eric, whose deal was cocaine and he was just using Pete for his money. Put it this way, he certainly helped Pete to blow through his cash. I felt bad about Pete being taken advantage of, so the New York deal was kind of a mutually beneficial arrangement. I had to feed my habit and in the same trip was able to take care of Pete. God, I used to make that drive at least every two to three weeks.

Joanna and I had a mutual friend and I had run back into her in his guitar shop. I'd describe her as being a typical blonde girl, always upbeat, bubbly and happy-seeming. She was an extrovert like that, though at the same time wouldn't push herself to the fore, but hang back and be a little cooler. It was through her that I was introduced to Pete, and right off the two of us fell to being the best of friends. For sure, I knew about his history as a musician, but he didn't make that big of a deal of it, was just a regular guy.

The two of them lived in this really cool, Victorian-style house. It was a very characterful place, but not in the best part of town. The area they were in is known as Olde Town East and located right next to downtown Columbus. At one point it had been a good, upmarket neighbourhood, though that's going back quite a while. The Olde Town still had some nice residential streets even then, but the social demographic of the entire downtown had changed over time and some pretty terrible areas had come to surround it. By the time Pete moved in with Joanna, I guess in the vernacular of today that you'd call it the 'hood'.

Pete and I grew very close, so that I got to know him intimately. He's definitely quite the character. I knew about the amount of drugs he was taking, of course I did, because I was right there alongside him doing the same things. The room in the house where Pete and I spent most of our time became known as the Gary Lee Suite. I knew Joanna was using, too, but she kept it compartmentalized to a degree. I think she believed that she was fooling me, but I was around enough, and staying over at weekends, to be fully aware of their lifestyle together. For the most part, though, Pete and I would be off in the suite while Joanna was in her bedroom. Pete would go back and forth between us, kind of like an attentive doctor.

201

———

Back when I had lived at the house in Bounds Green with Phil and the guys and we were all doing Mandrax, I never had a comedown. It's so much different, though, when you're shoving something straight into your veins. And it was with heroin that I finally lost my grip on my drugs use. It got to the stage where I would sit up all night, feeling dreadful, and just be hanging on for the FedEx delivery the next morning. When my package arrived from LA, I would run to the door, literally tear the box open, demolish the cake with my bare hands to get at the little brown balls of heroin and cook them up on the spot. I'd quickly slipped into that routine, so much so that every spoon of our cutlery was burnt black from being held over the cooker. I tried to come off smack several times back then, or else to reduce the amounts I was taking, but heroin withdrawal is such a living hell I could never go through with it. It's like having the worst bout of flu you could ever conjure up in your nightmares. Your whole body aches; bones, muscles, even your eyelids. It also made my skin itch and crawl, so that I'd want to rip it off with my own fingernails. I once asked Gary to suggest something that would allow me to kick heroin but without the awful suffering, and he told me that he'd make another fortune if he could ever answer that question.

My man in LA eventually took advantage of me, and made off with my money and supply. For days after, I went through all kinds of horrors. It started with a headache, more like a migraine, then I got hot and cold sweats and began to shake uncontrollably. I couldn't keep any food down and had these terrible aching pains, night and day. I'd literally have to prise my fingers open in the morning they were so cramped, and was climbing the walls. There was nothing that would take the edge off it. I sunk a quadruple whiskey – no effect. I tried injecting liquid Valium – no effect. In the end, the only thing that would ease the agonies was another shot of heroin. It was just the most vicious circle, so I made the decision to not even bother trying to quit. Particularly with the amounts that Joanna and I were both taking in the end, a sudden withdrawal would be such a shock to the system that it might bring about a heart attack.

Eventually, Joanna and I were pretty much living together in just one bedroom of our big old house. I was our chief chef. Like a dutiful husband, I'd go down to the kitchen each morning to cook up our first hits, shoot mine, and then take a full needle back upstairs for Joanna. It was midwinter by then and we had an electric heater going night and day. Joanna was fascinated by old-time movie stars and vintage Hollywood glamour, so the TV would always be tuned to the Turner Classic Movies channel. She would pore over all these books on the subject as well, so that it felt to me as if my whole life was being lived in stark black and white. The other substance we began to use was the anaesthetic that Michael Jackson was on when he died – Propofol. It's a white, creamy, quite thick liquid used in hospitals for surgical operations. Joanna had access to a ready supply of it, because she would use it when she performed liposuction. Since it was thicker than morphine, we had to shoot it up using different, bigger needles, but the effect would be near-instant. One second you'd be wide awake and able to hold a conversation, the next totally out for the count. In fact, one of our party games would be to see how high we could count before the Propofol put us under. Of course, I was aware of the risks but I enjoyed the feeling I got from using it and Joanna was very careful to measure our doses. She also made sure that she was never fucked up when she had to go into work. She'd shoot up just enough heroin to smooth her over and get her through the day, but not an amount that would cause her to nod out. Of course, it was highly illegal for a physician to be using in the first place, but not unheard of either.

Just like I had come to do on the road, I developed a daily routine of my own. I'd wake up at 7 a.m. and have a shot of either heroin or morphine. Morphine was easier to fix up and had the same effect, so I began to use that more often. Then I would have a shot of liquid Valium and follow that up with a handful of slimming pills mixed with speed. And that, pretty much, would be the cocktail I'd give myself every morning before breakfast.

Geddy Lee: I remember Pete coming to see a Rush show in Columbus when he was living in the city. I hadn't seen him for many years at that point, but he really wasn't in great shape and that bothered me. Pete had always seemed to me to be one of rock's great survivors, but he looked as if he was going through his own private hell.

Neill Way: Personally, I wasn't at the time fully aware of the difficulties Pete had got into in Columbus. During that period, he wasn't very communicative with the family. But my mum in particular did get the sense that he'd perhaps fallen in with a bad crowd. My wife and I saw a lot of his daughter, Charlotte, who was a teenager by then, and she went out to stay with Pete and Joanna. When she came back, she told us that the two of them had barely looked after her or even shown her

around the place. Charlotte said that they were both pretty much out of
their heads for the entire week that she was there.

Joanna and I didn't have a relationship that was simply about
drugs. For instance, she encouraged me to get back in touch
with Charlotte, and that in turn led to Charlotte coming out
to Columbus to stay with us. Joanna welcomed her with open
arms. As you'd expect of a doctor, she was able to hide her
addiction very well, but Charlotte's presence made things a
little more awkward for me. At regular intervals, I'd have to go
off for what I told her was a lie-down.

We had promised to take Charlotte to Walt Disney World
in Orlando. The three of us flew down to Florida, I rented
a car and we drove to Joanna's parents' place. Joanna and I,
though, ran out of opiates so I spent most of the two days we
were there in bed. The last thing I wanted to do as I came off
heroin was wander around the Magic Kingdom and have to
meet Mickey Mouse. So we got Paul Chapman's son, Tyson,
who lived nearby, to take Charlotte instead. I think the two of
them had a good time.

———

After the abrupt conclusion to UFO's last American tour, relations between Phil and Michael remained frigid for a long time.
With the band out of action, Phil and I decided to go off and
make a record together as Mogg/Way – not, it has to be said,
one of rock and roll's most memorable handles. We recorded
Edge of the World in a little town just outside of San Francisco.
The two of us had signed to an independent American label,

Shrapnel Records, and the owner, Mike Varney, was also act-ing as our producer. Mike, who is a big, bald bear of a man, picked Phil, Joanna and me up from San Francisco Airport. I had tried to keep my heroin use from Phil, but from the moment we touched down in California that proved to be near enough impossible.

Joanna and I had travelled with our two cats and my little Pomeranian dog, Princess. Joanna had also brought along with her a prescription for morphine. Phil was jet-lagged and dozed off in Mike's car just as soon as we pulled out from the airport, but woke to find Princess on his lap and that we had parked up outside a hospital. Joanna and I had gone inside to get two weeks' supply of morphine, no questions asked. Phil was pissed off at me, and quite rightly. That was the point, I think, at which a rift started to open up between us.

Nonetheless, Phil and I also had some good times making that record. Twenty minutes' walk from the house we were renting was a little liquor store that was run by an elderly Korean couple. They stocked an American kind of champagne, a sparkling wine called Cook's. It was a nice, refreshing drink, and Phil and I couldn't get enough of the stuff. Each morning, I would walk down to the store and pick up two or three bottles of Cook's for the two of us to drink during the day. Later on in the evening, Phil would drive down and get three or four more bottles for that night. This went on for the whole month that we were in town. By the time we left, the floor area of the basement, a space the size of a squash court, was filled with empty Cook's bottles. There must have been 200 of them at least. And that proved to be very good for our new Korean friends. In the last week of our stay, the local Cook's rep visited the store to tell them they had won the company's monthly sales competition for the area and a free holiday to Hawaii. The two of them were very pleased with us.

Edge of the World got some positive reviews, but it was inevitable that UFO would return to action. The shows that we *had* managed to do on the *Walk on Water* tour had been so successful that we got lots of offers to carry on. The largesse of these finally persuaded Phil and Michael to gloss over their differences and we hit the road again at the start of 1998. However, by then I was a fully-fledged junkie. I tried to cover it up by telling the others I was on a course of steroids, but soon enough got caught shooting up on our tour bus.

I had meant to hide myself away on the upstairs deck, but was quietly fixing up when Paul Raymond unexpectedly appeared. Paul spied what I was up to, which had never been part of his agenda, and began to loudly berate me about how horrible it was for him to see. It wasn't my finest moment, that's for sure. And by the end of the American leg of the tour, our tour manager had also got on my case. At that juncture, I'd dropped to just nine stone in weight.

I was doing so much smack it took precedence over everything else in my life, including groupies. In part that was because I didn't want anyone coming into my hotel room and seeing me fix up. To be frank, I had also all but lost my sex drive. As a result, I found myself on my own quite a bit. The others in the band tended to steer clear of me, Paul in particular. For them it must have been like touring with Count Dracula. Most nights, I'd retreat to my room, shoot up and nod out. The room would be in a dreadful state, with all of my clothes strewn over the floor, along with my needles, spoons and general drug detritus.

All that I was bothered about was my next shot. And at the height of my using on that tour, I'd have to shoot up as often as ten times a day. I would also have to time each one just right, so that I didn't doze off onstage. Generally, I preferred to have one or two big bottles of methadone with me rather than heroin. Joanna was able to write out a prescription for me in her maiden name, which stated it was necessary for me to transport methadone, as well as morphine and needles. That did the job in most countries we visited and I was able to slide right on through customs, but not in Japan, where you aren't allowed to bring in any drugs at all.

We flew out to the Far East straight from doing a show in Palo Alto, California. I had smuggled a stash of smack onto the plane, and shortly before we came into land went into the toilet to shoot it up. Since at the time we were being tossed around in turbulence, it was tremendously difficult for me to find a vein. Again and again I tried to stick the needle in as the plane was thrown this way and that. It had a comical side to it, I suppose. But thank God I managed to do it in the end, because the customs officials at Nagoya Airport subsequently treated me like a smuggler and I was taken off and strip-searched.

I'd hoped to ride out the storm of withdrawal in Japan, but every minute of our five-day visit was like a living death for me. The whole time, it felt as though I had insects crawling under my skin and that my body was screaming in protest. Despite this, it wasn't me who caused yet another of our tours to crash to an undignified halt. We had been booked to play three nights at the Sun Plaza Hall in Tokyo, which held upwards of 5,000 people. Every ticket had been sold, which meant a million dollars a night in gross profits. People had even flown in from Australia, New Zealand and all parts just to see us.

The first night, Michael cracked up. Three songs into our set, he smashed his guitar, stormed off stage and refused to go back out. He claimed that he just couldn't take being in the band any more. Our promoter, a courteous but officious gentleman named Mr Udo, made me go out and apologize to the bewildered audience. Next morning, the insurance people turned up at our hotel. All that Michael had to do for them to agree to cover the costs of the gig was to say that he had felt ill, because the doctor in attendance was part of Mr Udo's entourage. What Michael said instead was: 'The reason I walked off is that I fucking hate the people I am working with.'

Of course, we had to pull the remaining dates. Phil claimed he'd rather play phone boxes for the rest of his career than go through that again. We'd always known that anything was liable to happen with Michael, and had never at any time been entirely sure of his mental state. Passing up three million dollars, though, was a pretty good indication that all was not well in his head. For Phil, Andy and I it was just like the first time we'd visited Japan with the *UFO 1* album. Once again, we left the country in disgrace. This time, we had flown in first class and had two stretch black limos ferry us from the airport. We got sent off in a people carrier and flown home at the back of the plane.

After that debacle, there was nothing for Phil and me to do but to make a second Mogg/Way record. However, *Chocolate Box*, as we eventually called it, was much more of a challenge for me than our first effort had been, since I had to shoot up almost on the hour just to stay on an even keel. Even Phil

209

was shocked. He'd known from the UFO tour that I was a regular user, but even then hadn't grasped the full extent of my addiction. There were days in the studio when I wasn't able to continue playing, because my hands would start to cramp up. I'd have to stop and ask Mike Varney to run me back up to the house so I could get my fix. I don't think that Mike had ever before had to perform that service for one of his clients. He'd sit outside the house in his Mercedes while I popped in, whacked in a load of morphine and then ran back out to the car. And that would be enough for me to be able to finish the take. Phil got to be incandescent with rage at me, and I could hardly blame him. Even I had begun to sense that I was in serious trouble.

CHAPTER 14

*Concerning the tragic, but all-too-predictable moment
when all of the chickens came home to roost.*

———

Gary Lee*: It was never Pete that I feared for. My own perception of
reality might have been distorted at the time, but Pete didn't appear to
me to get too crazy with the drugs. I mean, he wouldn't take things too
far in the sense of doing a dangerous amount of heroin in one shot. He
was, of course, using needles, so yes, there was always the risk of an
overdose and I suppose I worried about how much damage he was doing
to himself with all of that poking about in his veins.*

*Crazy as it might sound, it was Pete's drinking that used to concern
me way more than the drugs. It's a proven fact that habitual use of
alcohol over many years is way worse for you than even heroin. Not
that I'm endorsing heroin here, but Pete would drink a lot.*

I flew straight home to Columbus from Japan. My good friend
Gary had bought us a fresh supply of China White back from
New York, and after the horrors of the preceding few days

that news was like manna from heaven for me. Whenever I returned from the road, Joanna and I would always have a huge celebration together which would inevitably finish up being a case of needles-are-us. Even then, no matter what depths we had sunk to, I couldn't bring myself to pull us back from the abyss.

However, in the back of my mind I always knew there was the possibility of one of us overdosing. I came very close once or twice, but never did. Generally, I was careful to take heroin in manageable quantities. And because I used several times each day, for me it had come to be like having a half-pint of cider every three hours, or at least that's what I told myself. I was beyond the point of trying to get high, though, that's for sure. I knew that was a fool's game.

Being at something of a loose end yet again, I turned back to my music and began to write songs. I'd still be up each morning at seven to cook up as usual, but just as soon as I'd banged in my shot, I would head outside to the garden with a guitar and play for a couple of hours. I ended up with a bunch of songs that I was pleased enough with that I wanted to record them for posterity. And Gary not only kept me supplied with the means to get through the process, but was also the inspiration for how my first solo album, *Amphetamine*, came to sound. He'd often play me classic American punk rock, bands such as the Stooges and MC5, and I grew to love the naked aggression of their music. In UFO, we had once more lost our edge, gone a bit Barry Manilow here and there. By complete contrast, I wanted *Amphetamine* to be very basic and in your face.

Combined, the songs themselves were like a film script about my life at that time. There was one song, 'Hole', for example, that detailed how desperate I'd been waiting for the

FedEx truck to pull up outside the house. Others were about some of the people I'd got to know in what the locals called the black ghetto of the city. If you were to walk just a hundred yards from where we lived, you'd find yourself in one of the gang territories. And on a couple of occasions, I got arrested in that part of town.

First time, I was pulled over in my car for driving erratically and had coke on me. I was thrown in one of those big holding cells you see in the movies, with twenty or so other guys, most of whom were black. To start with, they tried to intimidate me, called me 'white boy'. But once I told them I was a musician, they let up. In actual fact, they mistook me for Tommy Lee and one or two even asked me for my autograph. Second time, I had driven down to the liquor store in my latest car, a mint condition Coupe de Ville '64, which had a couple of speeding tickets on it that I'd forgotten to pay, having gone off on tour. The cops spotted me, impounded the car and whisked me off downtown again. I ended up going to court on that charge, but got off.

In respect of that ordeal, being a member of UFO did have its advantages. The day I turned up at the courthouse, my lawyer pulled me to one side and asked why I hadn't told him I was famous. He told me the presiding judge wanted me to sign something for his wife and also to ask me about the recording of 'Rock Bottom'. It turned out that the judge and his wife had met at college and in their student days had listened to UFO records together. Not only was the charge against me dismissed, but I also got handed $500 in compensation.

The Columbus county jail could actually be quite pleasant if you were in there with the right people. It was a well-scrubbed,

213

modern building and tended to house guys who had done daft things rather than mass murderers. Though I did get told by one guy that if I was ever to do a bank robbery, I had to make sure I was in and out of the place in under a minute. That was good to know, obviously. All it needed was a bar and I'd have been happy enough to stay over. Each time I was arrested, Joanna had to come down to the jail in the middle of the night to bail me out. Afterwards, I got to know a couple of the gang guys I'd met in there and was able to hook them and their girlfriends up to see her as a doctor, free of charge, since none of them could have ever afforded medical insurance. It seemed to me as if there were always fights going on between them and they were also caught up in a continual turf war with another gang. On more than one occasion, I watched someone load up a Smith & Wesson revolver and head off round the neighbourhood. Sometimes, I'd see a guy on the street one day and he'd be gone the next.

If I'd been a white American I'm sure they would have been thoroughly hostile towards me, but I think I got treated differently because of the fact I was English. In a way, I was a novelty for them and we even sort of became friends. Quite often, I'd go and hang out at their places, or else invite them up to our house. If they came to ours, I'd get them to listen to my songs and give me their opinion. I don't think one of them was older than their twenties and all they listened to was hip-hop, but I think they liked the element of truth in what I was doing. And that record was all too true. There were an awful lot of good musicians in Ohio and I got a couple of local guys to play on the album with me, a guitarist named Walt James and Scott Phillips, a drummer. We rehearsed in the ballroom of the house and recorded down in the basement. It finished up being a great album, and one I still take a lot of pride in. The problem was I put it out through a small record label and it wasn't made widely available. Very sadly, the Pete Way curse also struck yet again through the making of *Amphetamine*. The two guys I had got to engineer the record for me both ended up dying of overdoses. Wherever I went back in those days, there was a certain amount of drugs being supplied, and unfortunately it seemed to be the case that I unwittingly encouraged a number of people to go beyond their limits.

Eventually, Joanna and I decided to make plans to get out of Columbus. The neighbourhood was deteriorating and she wanted to move closer to her parents in Florida. In the meantime, we sold up and moved into a rented place in the city. It was another big house, set on four floors. One of our first visitors was the guitarist, Joe Bonamassa. Joe hadn't yet released his first record, but was being talked about as the best young blues guitarist in the States. UFO's booking agent in America believed he would be the perfect replacement for Michael in the band, so arranged for him to fly to Columbus and for the two of us to meet. We ended up jamming for a night in my basement and got on great, though it must have been weird for him to have me disappear upstairs every ten minutes to get my fix. At all events, he didn't in the end join UFO.

Joe Elliott also came round late one night after Def Leppard had played in town. I can't have made a great impression on that occasion either and didn't even try to make a secret of the fact I was shooting up. In fact, short of me sitting there with a needle dangling out of my arm, I couldn't have made it any more apparent that I was by then a full-blown junkie.

Joe Elliott: I remember very well hanging out with Pete in Columbus. He'd set up a kind of shitty little studio in this bloody awful basement of his and had all his gear down there. There was nothing on the walls but this damp, black, coal-like dust and it was fucking freezing. It looked like he'd dug it out with a spade. Pete wanted the two of us to write a song, but he was too far gone to do anything. He was just nodding out all the time. The thing is that Pete sparkled as a true rock star, and he's made a lasting impression on people's lives, but he always was destined to burn bright and then fade. That's just the way it goes.

Mike Clink: It was pretty much common knowledge in the business what Pete was going through. People would talk. Knowing that I had worked with UFO previously, they would tell me that he was not doing at all well and then again that his problems had elevated to a whole other level.

Eventually, even my parents became aware of the severity of my addiction. Joanna and I went over to stay with them in Essex for a week. While we were over there they took us to a big family lunch at my Uncle Brian's and Aunty Barbara's house, both of whom had come to watch me play as a teenager and were delighted to see me again. They had laid on a lavish spread and everyone sat down together to eat, but all Joanna and I did was pick at our food.

Every ten minutes or so, the two of us would have to excuse ourselves to go to the bathroom. Of all things, I claimed that the zip on my trousers had burst and that I needed Joanna to help me to fix it. Of course, no one believed that. My parents, though, didn't say anything to me about it at the time. I think they preferred to pretend that everything was all right, even though I had dropped so much weight that I looked positively skeletal.

Stupidly, I didn't even mind that for a time, because it meant I was able to wear anything I wanted. It was as if I could keep myself in trim without ever having to go to a gym. However, once I got past that point of vanity, and got thinner still, it slowly began to dawn on me that I couldn't keep on doing this to myself, that sooner or later there would be a heavy price for me to pay. There are, though, millions of addicts just like me who have sworn that they aren't going to have another shot, or snort, or drink tomorrow, but still do so regardless, over and again.

Sometimes, the sheer chemistry of it alone would be a distraction to me. Joanna began to work on a theory that if we took enough beta-blockers to slow our heart rates down, we would be able to do as much coke as we liked. Scientifically, she worked out the absolute maximum amounts of both that we should be able to take if we were injecting the coke to prolong the rush. It was, though, a very high-risk strategy and Joanna had a couple of seizures testing it out. On the first occasion, I made the mistake of calling for an ambulance. I didn't mention that Joanna was a doctor and managed to get her out of the seizure before it arrived, but she woke to find herself surrounded by medics. At the time, Joanna had been reading a book with very small print and the medics suggested it was that which must have brought her seizure on, or at least that was how they were happy to pass it off. Joanna told me afterwards in no uncertain terms that I was never to ring for medical assistance again, since there was a serious risk of her losing her licence to practise. Looking back now, that should have been the least of our fears.

———

The state of things in UFO had slipped into a familiar, depressing pattern. At some point or other after one of Michael's escapades, the dust would eventually settle and we'd all agree to give it another go. So it was that at the start of the new millennium Michael was coaxed back and we made yet another comeback album together, *Covenant*. It had its moments as a record, but no more than that, and didn't sell beyond our dwindling band of hardcore fans.

That November, we embarked upon a European tour with Aynsley Dunbar on drums, which passed off without incident. Next, we lined up eight UK shows in the lead-up to Christmas and Joanna flew over to be with me for those. Sadly, the whole enterprise was a rotten misadventure. The trouble started after the second show at Newcastle City Hall. Earlier that evening, I'd had an argument with Joanna, after which she'd stormed off, so I took the first car back to the hotel to smooth things over with her. I saw that Spike from the Quireboys had come backstage to say hello to us, but left him to Phil and wasn't made aware that anything untoward had gone on until two the next morning.

At that time, I went downstairs to order a drink from the night porter on reception. As we were passing the time of day, he told me that one of my colleagues, a Mr Schenker, had not long returned from hospital in an ambulance. Presumably, Michael, however stricken, had also stopped off at reception to pick up a drink. The next morning, I spotted Michael in the hotel bar. Just from the fact he was drinking, I knew all was not well. Upon closer investigation, I saw that he had a black eye and had written above his eyebrow in a gold felt-tip, 'Spike did this'. That was a pretty good indication of how the rest of that day was going to go. By the accounts of others in the band and crew, the previous night Phil had been waiting with Spike and Spike's uncle for his car from the venue. For some unfathomable reason, Michael convinced himself that since the three of them were in a huddle, they must have been talking about him. I was told that he stormed over to them, making a beeline for Spike, who of course suggested that he piss off. Michael then went to throw a punch, but Spike got there first and laid him out. As Phil once said to me, never pick a fight when you're drunk. In the melee that ensued, Phil tried to hold Michael on the floor and get him to calm down. Eventually, though, the police were called. Now, Spike's a local Geordie lad and treated like a national treasure up in Newcastle, so the coppers were not about to argue when he pleaded self-defence; in any case, Phil backed him up. However, it was muggins here who had to drive down with Michael from Newcastle to Manchester for the next show. Michael still had 'Spike did this' written over his eye, but made an effort to appear cheerful to me. It was obvious, though, that he was seething inside. From Michael's point of view, the dust-up could not possibly have been his fault, it never was.

Even for us, the show that night at the Manchester Apollo was catastrophic. Starting with our second number, Phil would attempt to introduce a song only to have Michael walk right up to him and shout in his face, 'You are a cunt!' I tried on several occasions to calm Michael down and Phil did his best to ignore him, but it was so obvious what was going on that people in the crowd began to take sides, and mostly against Michael. All of a sudden, Michael began to get all of this stuff thrown up at him from the stalls: half-empty plastic cups of beer, cigarette ends, even coins and lighters. That, of course, was it for another tour and we cancelled the remaining dates. Funnily enough, Michael had wanted to soldier on to the bitter end, but Phil swore he would never set foot on a stage with him again, a promise that he has stuck to ever since.

Michael Schenker: What can I say, but lots of promises made to me got broken around that time. Phil Mogg would change his mind about everything and then nothing about the band worked any more. It was no help to me that Pete was in such a mess as well. Basically, he was all over the place in every aspect of his life and I was helpless to do anything for him.

Joanna and I flew back to the States together, but I simply wasn't able to think straight. My US residential visa had run out and before we left London I was supposed to have gone to the American Embassy in Grosvenor Square to pick up a new one, but it had clean slipped my mind. When we landed at LaGuardia Airport in New York, I wasn't allowed back into the country. Joanna was livid with me and had to go off to a hotel on her own. I, meanwhile, was kept locked up with groups of Vietnamese and Filipino people, all of whom were waiting to be deported. The customs officials were actually very apologetic towards me, and even let me make a call to Joanna at the hotel. That didn't go so well either. One of the officials dialled the number for me and informed Joanna that he had her husband with him. Joanna initially refused to speak to me, but did relay through him that I was, and I quote, 'fucking doomed'. Eventually, I managed to get her on the phone and tell her that I was being flown back to London, but I assured her I would then pick up my visa and get the first plane out to the US. We didn't, though, part on good terms.

Back in London, I got the visa at last and was finally able to book a flight home for Christmas Eve. Bugger me, I then went and missed the plane. The roads were horribly congested with holiday traffic and my taxi got stuck fast, so we arrived at Heathrow just minutes too late. Joanna and I had at least made up by then and spoken on the phone a couple of times a day. I tried to get hold of her from the airport but there was no answer. I ended up having to spend Christmas Eve night in the terminal and on Christmas Day managed to get booked onto an Air France flight to New York, but out of Paris.

Once more, I tried to reach Joanna when I landed in Paris, but again without success. Her not being at home on Christmas Day made me truly fearful for the first time. I actually hoped that she had run off with someone else, rather than the alternative. I arrived into JFK Airport and was still not able to get hold of Joanna from there. So I called my local coke dealer in Columbus and asked him to pick me up from my connecting flight. The one blessing to having handed over so much of my money to him was that he was happy to oblige me.

He drove me to the house. The lights were on inside, but the front door was locked and I knocked but got no answer. I was forced to break in and knew straight away that something was terribly wrong, because our two dogs were roaming the stairs and had obviously not been fed. I walked up three flights and found Joanna in our bathroom. She was laid out on the tiled floor, rigid and blue. I tried to give her the kiss of life, but of course it was hopeless. She had lain dead like that for two days. Any junkie will tell you that something like this can happen at any time, and throughout that journey I had mentally prepared myself for the worst, but I was nonetheless in a state of utter shock. The image of Joanna lying dead in my arms has not left me and never will.

I called the cops, who came to the house and examined the scene. I had my flight ticket from New York on me, so it was apparent to them that I had not been at home at the time of Joanna's death. Joanna had got a load of coke and morphine in the house. There was a big pile of coke tipped out on a mirror at the top of the stairs. The cops took the mirror with them as evidence, but spilt most of the coke on the floor. After they had gone, I got down on my hands and knees, sobbing, and snorted it up from the steps.

Ever since, of course, I have run over endlessly in my mind what might have happened in our house while I was in London. No doubt, Joanna was lonely because it was the Christmas holidays. She may have had people over, but she was a very private person, didn't like to be disturbed, and more likely she would have spent the time on her own up in our bedroom. Her death was headline news in Columbus. The autopsy showed that she had taken massive amounts of cocaine and a local paper speculated that it was a suicide, but I don't for a second believe that to have been the case. The report went on to suggest that she had been worried about money, but we had $150,000 in just one of our accounts, so that wasn't an issue. From all I know, I believe that Joanna had again been experimenting with beta-blockers and cocaine, and as a result had suffered a third and fatal seizure. Just as I would do later on with Bethina,

I agonized over whether I could have saved Joanna, but I think not. Had I been there her death might have been prevented, but it was a tragedy in waiting. Joanna was a binge user and as such always in danger of going too far. A friend of mine got her father on the phone for me and I broke to him the news of her death. Joanna's dad was a retired doctor and very proud that his daughter had followed in his footsteps. It was awful for me to hear the hurt and disbelief in his voice.

He had, though, known what was going on with us in Columbus. Just recently, Joanna and I had spent a week at the family home in Florida. After we left, her parents had found a stash of used needles in the room we'd shared. Neither of us had been bothered to get rid of them. Her family stayed in Florida rather than come to Columbus for her funeral. I think they preferred to grieve in private.

I organized the service myself and thought the best way to send Joanna off was to try and make it a joyful event, more of a celebration of her life. Afterwards, the undertakers told me that it was the best funeral they'd ever put on. All of us, mourners and employees, went out back in the funeral parlour, where the coffins were kept, and snorted lines of cocaine off a tabletop. I had bought champagne for everyone to toast Joanna, and then went back to a friend's house and found oblivion in yet more booze and cocaine.

CHAPTER 15

*Yet further down the spiral, including our hero's grim
revelation that his veins were beginning to leak.*

———

Neill Way: *Pete wouldn't let it show, that's not the way he is, but he was
badly affected by Joanna's death. And I know that Mum and Dad were
very concerned that he would end up doing something stupid to himself.*

After Joanna's funeral, I cleaned out her office and drove down
to Florida with all of her medical equipment and her ashes. Of
course, I was still in a pretty terrible state and took along a supply
of morphine to help get me through the journey. I got pulled
over by cops just outside of Kentucky for speeding. The cops
actually confiscated four or five syringes from the back seat, but
didn't search the rest of the car and I got off with just a ticket.

I left Joanna's ashes with her parents in Orlando and my inten-
tion had been to give all of her equipment to her younger sister,
Carol, who lived just up the road from them in Gainesville.
Carol was a lecturer at Florida State University and I had

224

thought she'd be able to find a home for it there. However, she didn't want to have anything to do with Joanna's stuff. Carol was of the opinion that Joanna had always been erratic and trouble, and the two of them had not spoken to each other for several years.

Carol, though, invited me to stay on a while with her in Florida. That brief interlude in Gainesville was very healing for me. Carol and Joanna were alike in a number of respects, and not just physically, since both were highly intelligent and had somewhat eccentric personalities. In those few weeks together Carol and I forged a close, platonic relationship which endured for many years.

Eventually, though, I drove back up to Ohio. I had carried on bingeing on coke while I was in Florida, but didn't have the same close relationship with drug dealers there as I had in Columbus. In fact, pretty much everybody I had got to know in Columbus was by then hooked on heroin and we all of us hung out for the same reason. It was like a little medical club. We'd all shoot up together, nod out and then do it again. To me at the time, we were leading a bohemian existence and by comparison everyone else's lives seemed crushingly dull.

It was also true that the only way I could handle Joanna's death was to numb myself with drugs. After all, I had moved back into the house that Joanna and I had rented in the city, and slept, if at all, in the bed that we'd shared. I fell into a state of utter despair. As well as shooting up coke and heroin, I was using Demerol, which has a similar effect to morphine. Regularly, I'd stay up doing drugs for three days straight and not notice whether it was light or dark outside, lost as I was in my own narcotic fog. It didn't help that there was a lot of money available to me after Joanna died. Apart from the fact that we had sold our house, I had also received some life insurance cash. That which I didn't blow on drugs, I spent on cars. While I was still in Florida I bought a classic Dodge Viper, blood red and the fastest production car in the world. The Viper did nought to sixty in just two or three seconds, so people bought it ostensibly to race. I, on the other hand, bought it as a means of escape.

The first and only time I used the Viper to maximum effect was on the drive from Gainesville back to Columbus, going through the Blue Ridge Mountains in Virginia. I put my foot down and hit 150mph and more, not caring what might be coming over the hill or round the next bend. I otherwise reached a state where I ate, slept and did pretty much everything else on smack. During the spring that followed Joanna's death, that included being able to go back to work on a new album with UFO called *Sharks*. Really and truly, Joanna was my motivation to return to the band and try to get on with my career. She'd always been 100 per cent behind me in that respect. And with my music at least, I could never do any wrong in her eyes. Whether they recognized just how important it was to me I don't know, but Phil and Michael were even persuaded to work together once again, though it would be for the last time. Michael quit the band for good just as soon as we'd finished the record. The truth is, Michael's very proud of UFO but artistically temperamental and ill-suited to being in a group with Phil, especially, since neither of them will ever back down from an argument. In the end, I think they simply exhausted each other. Michael and I kept in contact, though, and when he found out that I'd been writing the songs for a planned second solo album, he offered me the use of his home studio. By then, he was living down in Scottsdale in Arizona, in a very well-heeled gated community, so he'd obviously been much more careful with his money than I had.

I flew down there from Columbus and spent a month or so staying in a mobile home on Michael's property. More than anything, I think Michael was concerned for my well-being after Joanna's death – but then, he always had kept one eye on his guitar and the other on me. Although I paid him for the studio time, the two of us built up a very strong bond during that period. To begin with, Michael intended just to play on my record, but then he suggested that we form an actual band together.

That band became the Plot, which also ended up being the title of the album we made in Scottsdale. The biggest compliment Michael's ever paid me was that he liked those songs of mine enough to want to put his name to them. I think he also got a lot of pleasure out of doing something that was different for him and the record proved to be reasonably successful. In the years that followed, the two of us got on better than ever, even became great friends. I played on two of Michael's albums, *Tales of Rock 'N' Roll* and *Temple of Rock*. In 2011, he also hired me to go out with the Michael Schenker Group on the tour he did for *Temple of Rock*. I would come out in the middle of their set and together we'd do two or three songs from *The Plot*.

Some things didn't change, though. Sadly, Amy Winehouse died while we were on the road and the next morning I asked Michael if he had heard the news. 'Yes,' he said very abruptly, 'and you will be next.' It was good to hear he hadn't lost his charm. Michael had, though, turned his own life around by then. He had quit drinking and was doing yoga and on the Atkins Diet. Indeed, before each show he would give the rest of us in the band a lecture on the benefits of clean, healthy living, which was just as much appreciated as you'd imagine. And when a couple of years after that he moved back to England and Brighton, I went to stay with him and we started to rehearse with the former Scorpions drummer, Herman Rarebell, with a view to starting yet another new band. To begin with, the three of us worked up a selection of old UFO and Scorpions songs and even alighted upon a name for our project, Strangers in the Night. Ironically, Phil had also by then moved down to Brighton and, to my astonishment, Michael suggested we get in touch and ask him to be our singer. Equally remarkably, Phil did actually drop by one day, but he'd been through so much with Michael that I don't think his nerves would take being in a band with him once again and so Strangers in the Night got shelved.

Michael Schenker: *Every time Pete and I worked together after I'd left UFO, the whole thing would ultimately just collapse. The Plot, for instance, turned out to be just that – a plot against me. I came up with the name, but somehow at the end of the project, Pete took the album and sold it himself. I didn't care about that, though; I'd wanted to help him in the first place.*

Later on, however, when I took him on the Temple of Rock tour, I couldn't even let him do a whole set with me. The truth was that he had become incapable of playing the bass. Time and again, I tried to help him. I called up his doctor and told him of my concerns for Pete, because it was clear to me that his physical health was getting increasingly worse. But in the end, I just wasn't able to rely on him and so there was no point for me in the two of us carrying on together.

For five, six years after Joanna died, I didn't care what drug I took, or how much, so long as I didn't have to think about tomorrow or the day after. I went through a small fortune on heroin, morphine and coke. If I wasn't high, I was depressed or else bored stiff. Eventually, I did get out of the rented house in Columbus, but only to move in with a woman who happened to be a drug dealer. The first time we met, it was 2 a.m. and she had on a pair of thigh-high, black leather boots from which she pulled a big bag of coke. I lived with her for the next six months. It was to my advantage not to have to pay full price for the huge amounts of coke I was doing, but she was also company for me because by then I had distanced myself from everyone I knew and got to feel dreadfully alone.

Naturally, my drugs consumption soon enough went into overdrive, to the point that I couldn't even recall what being straight felt like. A friend of my new housemate's, a black fella, used to freebase cocaine, and I thought the idea of smoking crack was the most appalling thing. He came round to our place one afternoon and was equally disgusted at the amount of coke I'd let drop on the carpet. It must have been a couple of grams that I'd wasted, as if I'd sprinkled it on the floor like a Shake n' Vac. He told me that with that same amount, he'd be able to use all day. Good luck to him – I let him scoop it up and take home. No matter how desperate things got for me, or how low I sunk, I just couldn't escape from the destructive cycle I was in. Eventually, blood even began to seep out from my needle wounds, here, there and everywhere. I had still got some really nice shirts and good suits that Joanna had bought

229

for me, but they all ended up being splattered with spots of blood. However, not even that shocked me to my senses. I simply applied antiseptic cream to each of the wounds and carried on regardless.

Eventually, living with a drug dealer got to be a bit much even for me. It seemed, therefore, an act of almost divine intervention when I met Rashida in a bar one night. Rashida was a young, tall, striking-looking black girl. She told me she had once been entered into the Miss Universe contest, which, whether true or not, will give you a good idea of the impression that she made on people. The two of us started to meet up every night for a drink and to play pool. Rashida lived with her parents in a big house in one of the better parts of the city, and it wasn't too long before she invited me to stay with her there in a guest room. In a couple more weeks, I'd moved my stuff again, into Rashida's room, and things carried on going just as fast between us.

In the end, though, I just got tired of living in Columbus. There were too many ghosts for me there, and so in 2003 I moved back to my old house in Birmingham but brought Rashida right along with me. I made the arrangements for her to study for a business degree at Aston University and, not long after, the two of us were married.

———

Neill Way: The Rashida wedding was the exception to the rule, in the sense that no one from the family, not even Mum and Dad, was invited.

To start with, it was a good marriage and I was an attentive husband. As a result of my drug habit, I was so used to remaining indoors that I never went off down the pub, or indeed anywhere else. As usual for me, though, it didn't last. I'm sure Rashida could very easily find fault with me, but from my perspective she became a bit of a control freak. She liked to be involved in every aspect of my life and to know each tiny detail. Also, she had a quick temper and an aggressive streak which would be multiplied if she'd had a drink. Her mother told me it was because she had Native American blood – she was part Cherokee on her father's side.

Gary Lee: Rashida fucking hated me. Apparently, the mere fact that I shared a surname with the Confederate Civil War general, Robert E. Lee, meant that I was somehow responsible for the whole fucking slave trade. I just knew from the start that she was bad news, but how are you supposed to tell that to your best friend about the girl he thinks he's in love with?

Garry Bushell: I thought Rashida was a terrific character, I must say. For some reason, Pete was always going on about her being a bloody Native American, but she was black, no question about it. She was bright and funny, but no, she couldn't take her drink. For Pete, that made for yet another bickering couple. And how shall I put this? Pete also has a reputation for stinginess – I mean to say, I've never known him to buy a drink. There was one time when he went out on tour and only took a single pair of trousers with him. Rashida went out and bought him two-for-the-price-of-one replacements on his credit card and they got into a massive row about it. He hit the roof, I'd never seen him so mad, and we're only talking about £50.

Thankfully, and as ever, I had my job to distract me from all of my personal problems. UFO made another album, *You Are Here*, with an American, Vinnie Moore, on guitar and Jason Bonham on drums. It was, though, a bit of a patchwork and it felt to me as if certain people were only now doing it for the money. The atmosphere was also fraught. Jason and I would argue over the most trivial of things. The fact was, he was in recovery from drug and alcohol use and I wasn't, but he'd grown up in a very different environment to me and I took offence at him lecturing me like a schoolmaster or else my father.

Phil was the one person who really kept a lookout for me and I still enjoyed being in a band with him. However, even he was starting to lose patience with me. I found the recording process difficult, because I was in such haze from all the drugs I was taking, and my playing was mediocre at best. Time and again, Phil told me that he didn't want me to die, but I either didn't want, or else just wasn't able, to listen.

And I still hadn't yet reached rock bottom. Later that same year of 2004, I found myself being back in touch with Fin Muir and the two of us started to write songs together again. That's just how it goes with musicians. Whatever might have passed between us, the best and most often the *only* way for us to communicate with each other is through the music we make. I suppose that's why we do it in the first place; otherwise we wouldn't be able to function. Fin had moved to Milton Keynes and I went to lodge with him for a few weeks. It got me out from under Rashida's feet at least and the upshot was that we reformed Waysted. Unfortunately, there was an off-licence at the bottom of Fin's street that opened its doors at 8 a.m. At 7.55 a.m. precisely each morning, Fin and I would set off on foot to get our first supplies of Special Brew together with several bottles of wine for the day. It was a very similar scenario to that of Phil and me in San Francisco with the Cook's champagne, but with even more unedifying results.

Each night before, Fin and I would have sunk an ocean of lager and wine, so the Special Brew run was our hair of the dog. On the walk back up to his house, we would each pop open a can and guzzle it down in one. Regrettably, our path took us past the entrance to the local primary school at the very time when scores of mothers were dropping their children off at the gates. It was the middle of winter, the two of us wore long, tattered overcoats, and for the poor parents and their offspring, it must have been like being confronted by a couple of tramps from the park.

There was, though, one particular morning that Fin and I were in an even worse state than usual. We took our first gulp of Special Brew and right there, directly in front of the school gates, in unison vomited it right back up. I have a clear, painful memory of a horrified line of mothers staring at us, mouths agape, and I shudder to think how wretched we must have seemed to them. After that incident, we did at least take an alternative route home but, once there, I would then have a bottle of wine for my breakfast. I was also using cocaine and downers in perilous amounts. And so Waysted's comeback album, *Back from the Dead*, was neither much fun to make nor very accurately titled. Indeed, there were a few occasions when I could very easily have died as a result of combining all that booze with sleeping pills, but I was by then utterly beyond the point of rational thought. In fact, it probably would have been for the better if I hadn't tried to revive Waysted. We weren't able to generate much interest in the band or attract any significant financial support, so neither *Back from the Dead* nor the last album we made together, *The Harsh Reality* in 2007, proved to be worth the time spent on them. To be truthful, though, there wasn't very much that was good about my life during that particular period.

Garry Bushell: At that stage, Pete's bladder wouldn't last a full live set. The UFO guys used to have one of the roadies stood in the wings and he was the keeper of the golden goblet. Pete would drink from a bottle of wine on stage, come off during a song and have a pee in the goblet, and then repeat for the whole show. The gag used to be that he might as well have drunk from the goblet, because what came out of him was pure alcohol.

One time, I convinced Pete and Micky Geggus from the Cockney Rejects to play a gig with my band, the Gonads, up in Leeds. We billed ourselves as the Unidentified Cockney Gonads and en route to the North picked up Pete from the train station at Milton Keynes. He'd been waiting there just half an hour for us, and a mate had given him two grams of coke for the journey. Pete told us that in the short time he had been sitting there, it was as if this bag of coke had started calling out to him, imploring him to dive in, and so he'd done the lot. Two grams of Charlie in thirty minutes!

It wasn't yet eight in the morning, but Pete wanted us to take him for a breakfast of Special Brew. Now, Phil Mogg liked a drink, too, but was always moaning about Pete's drunkenness. Matter of fact, all the two of them ever did was bicker. Throughout that day, I was getting calls from Phil to check up on Pete. And every time my phone rang

Pete would quite literally plead with me: 'Whatever you do, don't tell him I've touched a drop.' Yet even in the state he was in, it was still magical to watch Pete work. He was a fantastic bass player, more like a lead guitarist, so strutting and forceful, and such an important figure from that era of hard rock.

Not long after, I met up with Pete for a drink in my local. As he was sitting there, I couldn't help but look at his hands. They were so swollen it was if he were wearing gloves. There wasn't a vein in his body he hadn't exhausted by that point. He pulled up his trousers and showed me his legs, which were so scarred he looked like a shrapnel victim. It was horrible. Truly, I have no idea how he is still alive.

For all the difficulties I had and the pain I was causing to myself and others, there are still moments that I look back on with fondness or else amusement. I remember one gig in particular that UFO did on a cruise ship sailing from Helsinki to Stockholm. It seemed a good idea when it was put to us and we got paid very well for our trouble, but the night of our show, I was enduring the nightmare of methadone withdrawal and looked beyond awful. Somehow or other I got through our set, but by 1 a.m. the next morning I was again climbing the walls. I had by then sunk fifteen vodkas but that still hadn't dulled the pain, and though I felt as much like eating as throwing myself in the North Sea, in my desperation I decided to give food a go. Outside the cabin, the ship was still lit up like bloody Las Vegas, which made my head throb and eyes hurt. I made my way, though, to the self-service cafeteria and joined a queue of other insomniacs. Keep in mind now, I hadn't bothered to change from the gig and was still wearing mascara.

After a couple of minutes of waiting, a middle-aged Finnish guy tapped me on the shoulder and said very loudly, 'Excuse me, transvestite, but is this the line for food?' It was only because I couldn't have felt less like Lennox Lewis that I didn't grab him by the throat and hurl him overboard.

———

I was able to make just one more – and once again not-so-great – album with UFO: *The Monkey Puzzle*. We toured Europe to support it, but then I got fired from the band. In part at least it was the same old story. There was a kerfuffle over money, which wasn't my doing. It was also the case that Phil had given me an ultimatum: to stop using or to go. Rightly so, to be fair to him, because by then I was just about a wreck and not able to play at all well.

However, the situation got to be extremely petty. Phil also had a go about the state of my hotel room and I got a silly letter from Paul Raymond griping about my general behaviour. I didn't need to be ordered about. After all, *I* had started the band in the first place. The final straw, though, was that I got turned down for a work visa for the subsequent American tour. I failed the necessary medical on account of not being able to give a blood test. The veins in my arms were so damaged from all the times I had shot up into them that the nurse wasn't able to extract any blood. That was regarded among the management and my fellow band members as being the ultimate sin. I tried to hire a lawyer to appeal against the decision, but his services would have cost me £500 an hour and often as not such cases can take up to a year to resolve. In the meantime, the others went off and did the tour with a stand-in bassist. Since my name was still on the tickets, though, it was agreed that I would receive a percentage of all the merchandise sold on the tour. No sooner had the band completed the dates than Rashida began to call Phil incessantly and demand my money. Rashida could be obnoxious in the extreme, so much so that the whole affair was brought to an end by a very angry phone call from Phil to tell me that my services were no longer required.

Nearly ten years on, I realize now how disappointed Phil in particular and the rest of the band must have been in me. Quite simply, I'd let all of them down too many times. I did still try to give 100 per cent, but my body just wasn't up to the job any more. Sadly, Phil and I haven't spoken in a good while. In a way, he is like the other marriage in my life; we spent almost forty years together, so I was with him for much longer than any of my wives. At the time, though, I was so far gone I wasn't too troubled by being sacked. I told myself that I hadn't enjoyed being in the band for years, and it is a fact that we'd long ago stopped making our best music. I certainly wasn't going to call Phil back and offer to do a rehab. Today, I can admit that what I'd really grown sick of was my life as a whole. I had, at last, reached my lowest ebb and the point where I no longer cared about myself or anything or anyone else.

CHAPTER 16

*The road to recovery is located with the unexpected
assistance of a mallet, ruined groins and a
complete loss of pubic hair.*

———

I had to try and keep myself busy. No matter how bad things
had got for me, UFO had been my anchor, something for me
to hold fast onto, and now I was adrift and in peril. I didn't plan
ahead but lurched into a bunch of different things. There was
the work I did with the Michael Schenker Group, the second
Waysted comeback album and a record titled *Damage Control*
that I made with Spike on vocals and a guy called Robin
George, a guitarist who lived near me in Birmingham. None
of that, though, panned out. Often as not, the various projects
would end with there being bad blood and I'm not sure now
why I even did half of those things. I was just desperate for
something to do, I suppose.

In any case, I had other, more personal and serious issues to
try and resolve. I did one more stint in rehab for alcohol, but

again it didn't take. The advantage of being in those places is that you get to meet people from all kinds of different backgrounds, but not one of the actual treatments ever worked out for me in the long run. For the two weeks I was in a clinic, it would be nothing for me to go without booze. But then I'd come out and be left to my own devices once more.

On this last occasion, though, I didn't even manage to stay dry while inside. The place itself was nice enough, a country house just outside of Birmingham. But a couple of friends of mine came to visit me one afternoon and had decided I could use a pick-me-up, so kindly arrived with a six-pack of lager and a bag of coke secreted about their persons. It was the middle of summer and they had also worked out that we could sneak through a gap in the hedge at the bottom of the garden and make off down to the village pub. I didn't do the coke in the end, but in all other respects that was the end of that particular twelve-step programme.

It's all about willpower, isn't it? With booze, my ideal has always been to be able to have just a couple of glasses of wine with dinner, but I'm just not built like that. For me, booze is harder to kick than heroin. You don't have to go out of your way to get booze, for one thing. My brain also seems to be more effective when it's been a bit loosened. Still now if I'm trying to write a song and it's going horribly wrong, I have to fight the urge to think it will be better if I just have a drink; that the booze will give it a bit of oomph. These days, though, I do try to discipline myself with drink. I don't do spirits if I can help it, aside that is for an occasional Bloody Mary or two with my food. And admittedly, I do like to have a beer or cider by 10 a.m., but then again I wake up early. My day starts at six, so I look upon it as being the same as taking a drop with my lunch. That, to me, is not a habit, far from it, at least not when I think back on what I used to consume.

With heroin, it got to the stage where I simply couldn't get enough of it into me. It was no use if I bought a gram, because that would be gone in a day. Just to stay on a certain level, I had to shoot up almost all of the time. I was bound to die, but thank the Good Lord, fate intervened for me. The fact was, by then I couldn't get a needle into my arm or anywhere else even if I'd wanted to. In the end, I had to shoot up into my groin. I'd pretty much ruined the rest of my body by then. The groin is tough to get into, though, so I had to use a big old needle just so that it would penetrate the muscle. Soon enough, I also exhausted that option. Like most of my veins, those in my groin got to be so hard and calloused from scar tissue that I couldn't get even the big needle into them. So instead, I took to drinking methadone as if it were beer, glugging straight from the bottle. Actually, it's very sweet tasting and more like sherry, but oh dear, it can knock you for six. I once sank the best part of a bottle at a friend's house and was awake all that night hallucinating, but barely able to move.

Eventually, though, the scar tissue in my groin began to leak blood as well. Looking back, that was a blessing because it doubtless saved my life. The veins in both of my legs had got to be so full of holes that they'd collapsed. I was bleeding internally and down into my toes, so that my feet and ankles swelled up. At the time, I didn't know what was causing it so went along to Queen Elizabeth Hospital in Birmingham for a check-up.

Actually, the first thing the specialist told me was that he was the guitarist in the hospital band. They had a gig that coming weekend and he wanted to know if I would possibly go along and sit in with them. I made the excuse that I had other things on, which brought the conversation to an end. I had a full body scan, which was when it was found out that I was bleeding from the veins in my groin. Of course, I had to tell the doctor precisely what I'd been up to, meaning that these days, whenever I go for an appointment even with my GP, I can see the word 'Addict' written across the top of my file in bold lettering.

Since my condition was so advanced, the last resort was for me to have surgery. I had to have three veins removed from each of my legs and my groin area patched up. Having stuck so many needles into myself by then, I was only surprised that I hadn't caused a more serious and longer-lasting problem. The operation itself was a perfect success. I was up and out of there in a couple of hours, no obvious harm done. But then, to be forced into having your own veins extracted is a massive reality check and that was the end of the road for heroin and me.

My body had just said no. And on this occasion, no did mean no. I must have gone through a withdrawal when I came off heroin, of course I must, but not one that was so bad I can recall every detail. I was also prescribed something to help wean me off it, so it wasn't as if I went completely cold turkey. By then, too, I had got just enough common sense back to realize how bad things must have got for me to have been jabbing a needle into my crotch. Over the years, I'd spent thousands on heroin and my savings had gone down like sand through a timer. It's a cruel, merciless drug and it had near enough beaten me, but I wanted to get my life back.

241

I had also come to the realization that the way I'd carried on for so long hadn't been normal. It *wasn't* normal to have to spend a whole day in, say, Vienna trying to find a needle exchange. It *wasn't* normal to have to excuse myself from a room full of people to go to the loo and shoot up. And in the end, the best thing about smack proved to be getting off it.

———

If I had thought that kicking heroin would mean the rest of my life would run smoothly, I was soon corrected. Christmas has seemed to be a particularly bad time for me, and my next earthquake occurred on the Christmas Eve after my operation. Rashida and I were at home in Birmingham and had friends round for the night. They were two black girls who ran an occult shop just down the road from us, selling tarot cards, crystals and the like and to which I was a regular visitor. As the evening wore on, I kind of left Rashida and the pair of them to it and went upstairs to watch football on the telly.

Rashida, though, put some music on and all I could hear from downstairs was this loud, thumping noise. I didn't even like the record, whatever the hell it was, and shouted down to her two or three times to put something else on. Instead, it got even louder. Eventually, I went down and turned the stereo off. No sooner had I gone back upstairs, of course, than Rashida put it on again. Down I went once more and this time yanked the plug from the wall socket. And at this point, Rashida snapped and smashed me on the head with a mallet that she had been using to break nuts.

The wound immediately started to bleed all over my face so that I looked like something from a horror film. I was persuaded by the two girls to leave the house. They took me to their shop and wanted to call an ambulance. I wouldn't let them, since apart from a thumping headache I didn't feel too bad. Looking back now, I was probably concussed and not thinking straight. Later, the girls told me I was really stupid for not having called the police – they even took a photograph of my head to be used as evidence. I'm sure that, to them, the whole scene was awful, but what can I say? Both Rashida and I liked to have a drink and then we argued. That, though, was the end of my fifth marriage; inevitably, Rashida and I divorced. Today, I couldn't even begin to explain why it was that I kept on getting married. I don't know if it was stupidity on my part or that of my wives, but somehow or other it was always asked of me and I never declined. At all events, I moved out of my house and went to lodge with one of the girls from the occult shop.

During that same period, I also did the *Temple of Rock* album and tour with Michael and went on to stay with him in Brighton. In the back of my mind, though, I wanted to do something for myself once more. I started to write songs just for me, but was at a loss as to how to put my career back on the rails. I had, after all, burnt so many bridges by then it was almost as if I were an outcast, or worse still, seen as a hopeless case. It was my friend, Garry Bushell, who put me back in touch with Jenny Stanley-Clarke. I hadn't seen her for nearly thirty years, since she'd helped out Eddie Clarke and me with Fastway, but if Jenny didn't exactly save me, she did at the very least restore my faith in myself and got me up on my feet again.

Jenny Stanley-Clarke: *Oh, Pete needed to be saved and still does. Five years ago, he literally turned up on my doorstep in Bournemouth with a plastic carrier bag. It wasn't even filled with any of the things you would expect a normal person to bring along with them such as clothes, shampoo, or even a toothbrush. But it did contain several bottles, empties and otherwise.*

Pete looked completely different from the last time we had seen each other. I mean, if you had pointed this person out to me in a crowd and told me it was Pete Way, I wouldn't have believed it. Back in the day, he was fresh-faced, clean-cut and always immaculate in his appearance. The person who rolled up that day had hair just about down to his waist, which was so greasy it was like he hadn't washed it in months. He had the typical drinker's face, which is to say slightly bloated, and a big rip in his trousers around the crotch. And he only had the one front tooth. Honestly, he looked like a vagrant.

I had suggested that he come down from Birmingham just for the day, to see that we were both singing from the same hymn sheet. We went out for supper, but Pete just kept disappearing from the table. I assumed he was doing cocaine, but in fact he was going off for an illicit drink. My father was a drinker, too. He was a surgeon and I idolized him, but he vanished into a bottle of scotch and never came back out again. So I had been there, and that night I just completely fell in love with Pete. He blew my socks off. And I still have no idea why this person who you wouldn't really want near your children had that effect on me.

After the meal, we went back to my house and chatted until 2 a.m. Both of my sons were living with me at the time and so there wasn't a spare room. Pete ended up sleeping the night in my bed, and has never left. He informed me the next morning that he had hepatitis C, which was a worry from the point of view of my kids being in the house.

I instituted a big rule that Pete didn't use the same cutlery or glasses as anyone else. I knew, of course, what he'd been through with heroin and it was a challenge just to get him to appear decent, because the last thing addicts are interested in is how they look. My first stop with Pete was the hairdresser's. It was like dragging along a small child who doesn't want to have their hair cut. I also got him into a shower and bought him some trousers and a pair of trainers. Occasionally, he would go up to Birmingham and bring a few things back with him, stuff that he'd worn onstage. My view was that if he wanted to be a rock star again, he had to look and also act like one, too. In all, I had to put him back together piece by piece, because he was basically a man in tatters.

Mike Clink: For several years, Pete and I had been having the exact same conversation on the phone. It would typically be around dinnertime in LA, so 2 a.m. in the UK. I got used to him being very excited about some project or other, but nothing would ever come of it. He would tell me that he had all these great songs and then I wouldn't hear from him again for eight, nine months, when we'd go through the same routine.

Finally, it must be three years ago now, Pete called me up and we had our usual talk, but this time he did send me the material. And I just fell in love with it. It was the story of Pete's life in songs and that's what drew me towards really wanting to make a new record with him.

I sent Mike a tape full of songs and he called me back a couple of weeks later to tell me how much he loved them. He said he thought there was work still to be done on the tracks, but that he wanted to do it with me and for us to make an album together. To me, that moment felt like salvation, as if I'd been resurrected. Right then, though, I got stopped in my tracks yet again.

Not long before, I'd done an interview with *Classic Rock* magazine and the journalist had written about how often I went off to the toilet. I'm sure he thought I was doing coke, but far from it. The truth was my whole system had become irregular and I found that I needed to pee all the time. Often, it wasn't comfortable doing so, but I put that down to the after-effects of my operation and years of drug abuse. It was only when I noticed blood in my urine that I knew something else was wrong.

I had to see my doctor for a routine check-up anyway, so mentioned to him that I was peeing blood. He sent me straight off to the hospital down the road in Poole for further tests. The following week, I got a call from the hospital asking me to go along for a scan and to bring someone else with me. At the time, I didn't think twice about it. It was only later that I found out that when they ask you not to come alone, there is something serious they have to tell you.

Jenny went with me and, after the scan, a female doctor sat us both down in a small office, very matter of fact. She told me that I had prostate cancer, but that they'd caught it early before it had spread. I'd actually been very lucky. Prostate cancer is virulent and more often than not fatal if it isn't detected in time. I also didn't require surgery to remove my prostate gland, which is another likely eventuality and will leave you impotent. I was told that instead I would have to undergo radiotherapy, and Poole Hospital just so happened to be recognized as one of the best in the country for the treatment of cancer.

———

After I'd got the news, my first reaction was to go and have a beer. I mean, I hadn't been given a terminal diagnosis, so at that precise moment didn't give my cancer a second thought. I'd also had to endure even bigger blows than cancer. The previous year, we'd lost Dad. He had gone into hospital in Chelmsford with a heart problem, which he believed to be minor. He actually phoned Mum and told her he'd be out the next morning, instead of which she got a second call from the hospital to tell her that he had died overnight.

Mum went not too long after him, which of course is often the case. She had, at least, made it to ninety and Dad to his late-eighties. Perhaps there's something in the family genes that has kept me going. But no matter how old they get to be, you just don't believe your parents are going to die, do you? I thought both of them would get better, couldn't imagine them not being around. Even now, I still expect them to be there for me. I actually had a conversation with Dad in my sleep just the other night. It was about football and we had a good chat about some game or other.

On top of that, I was also going through the divorce with Rashida. It was much harder for me to handle Mum's death because of that happening at the same time. In fact, the divorce got so vicious that Rashida wouldn't even believe I'd got cancer. She claimed I'd made my illness up in order to help me get a better settlement. Taking all that into account, I suppose I got to feel quite fatalistic; that if it was my time to go then so be it.

Neill Way: *It's only more recently that Pete has got closer to the family. Gradually, and particularly as he broke away from Rashida, we began to see more of him. Dad's death hit him quite badly and he*

247

got really upset at the funeral. He admitted that he hadn't been around enough and said that he'd never properly got to know Dad. Afterwards, he was a lot more in contact with me and would go and see Mum as well. And when she went into hospital, he would come up every weekend with Jenny to visit her.

It was nice for me having a famous brother, but also difficult and frustrating. For many years, I didn't get to see or spend much time with him. We're very different characters. I like to have all the i's dotted, whereas Pete is thoroughly unreliable. Even now, I never expect to get a Christmas or birthday card off him, never mind a present. And there's been any number of times when Pete and a wife have been due to come to us at Christmas or for other family occasions, only for him to cancel at the last minute with a wondrous tale. For all that, though, he's a good brother. Around the time of his illness, I began to speak to him at least once or twice a week, and it's always good now to hear his voice and of his latest escapade.

According to my specialist, one of the things that had brought my cancer on was that I had too many male hormones. I was quite proud of that fact. It made me feel like John Wayne, or at least it did until I was told that I'd have to have female hormones injected in me to correct the imbalance. That treatment went on for weeks and the side effects started to worry me. For one thing, my voice went up an octave. Added to that, the doctors told me I might also grow breasts.

If I ever let the seriousness of my situation creep into my mind, I would get very down. Fortunately, at such times I was always able to find something else to think about or distract me. Some people find God at such times, but not me. I didn't even pray, not once. I found strength instead in humour. And you've got to have a sense of humour on a cancer ward, or else there'd be nothing for you to do but weep. In a way, I became almost the life and soul of the ward. I was the only patient who would turn up with a can of Special Brew, that's for sure. It wasn't as if I felt a kind of responsibility to be the joker, but I saw people hollowed out by leukaemia or with tumours on their faces and they were so obviously in a much worse condition than me. At the same time, they also fought their cancers with great dignity and I found that inspirational. If I could, by cracking a joke, or else telling one of my rock-and-roll stories, I tried not to let them dwell on things, if only for a moment.

I had targeted radiotherapy on my prostate for a month. An ambulance would pick me up from the house and take me to the hospital. I think there must have been some sort of competition to collect me, because I'd never have to wait for the ambulance to arrive. Often as not it would be ten minutes early and the crew would pop in for a coffee. One of the drivers told me that he'd Googled me and, after that, he would put on one or other of the UFO albums for the journey.

My treatment was actually a very easy process. I was laid down on a bed and covered with a towel, and the radiotherapy itself wasn't an unpleasant sensation, in fact it tickled. Each session would last just a few minutes and then a doctor would show me a scan so I could see how my tumours were responding. I had eleven tumours, which was obviously quite significant, but they were consistently reduced. I felt sick and drowsy after each treatment, but then so does everyone who undergoes it, and as mine was so specifically focused, I didn't go bald. Mind you, all my pubic hair fell out, which was a bit unfortunate.

249

Eventually, my cancer went into remission. Only a fool would fail to realize how lucky it is to be cured. Many times since, I have spoken to someone who's just been diagnosed with cancer and they've told me how they'll be fine. Four or five weeks later, I would be at their funeral. Maybe all the junk that I put into my body over the years toughened it up. Jenny was by my side for every one of my treatments and also during my darkest hours at that time. Essentially, we worked together on my recovery just as we had been doing on my career before I got ill. She had become my closest confidant and also my rock, and a year after I got the all-clear we were married. Obviously, my track record in that department is dreadful but someone's having the last laugh on me. Ever since having radiotherapy, things have been pretty much dormant for me downstairs, if you catch my drift.

Jenny Way [née Stanley-Clarke]: I don't know whether Pete brought out the mothering instinct in me, but I made it my job to look after him. To be honest, I still don't know what it is that I find attractive about him. He's utterly selfish and entirely self-absorbed, but then again, different to anyone else I've ever met. Truly, there's no one I know who's like him.

And I knew from the moment Pete came back into my life that we'd end up getting married; I had no doubts. Yes, I'm Pete's sixth wife, but he's also my fourth husband and I'm as tough as old boots. In fact, I often think of our relationship in terms of Henry VIII. It's like the old saying about his six wives goes: divorced-beheaded-died, divorced-beheaded-survived. There's been no beheading gone on in Pete's story, but there's certainly been the rest, so that in his case it's: divorced-divorced-died, died-divorced-survived. That makes me Catherine Parr, I guess, but who's to say?

For two years after I'd completed my treatment, I had no energy at all. In fact, I'd nod out just as often as when I was on smack. And at the hardest point of my recovery, I have to admit that I did dabble now and again with heroin once more, but I haven't touched it for more than three years now. Indeed, the last time I took an opiate of any description was over a year ago. At the time, I was suffering with cramps in my hands and legs, another side effect of heroin, to the point that it was doing my head in. Jenny keeps rabbits out in the garage and I remembered that she'd been prescribed some rabbit morphine for them. So I went out back and hunted around until I found the bottle. Then I popped it in a syringe and gave myself a little shot in the bum. It was a one-off thing, a bit like going to the doctor's except that I was able to treat myself. The cramps have eased up now, but my stomach is still getting over the treatment and is sore to this day, and I have a very difficult time controlling my bowels. However, if I moan to my doctor about this or about the fact I have to pee four or five times a night, he will simply point out to me that I have survived cancer and that I should eventually make a complete recovery. There are, of course, no guarantees that the cancer won't come back one day, but my last check-up was clear and that's good enough for me. There are tablets I could take for my bowels, but I would rather my body repair itself. That's an irony in itself, me not wanting to do drugs.

CHAPTER 17

Redemption songs . . .

———————————

Michael Schenker: *I never worried for Pete. He always used to say to me that life is what it is, and that's exactly the point. We all of us have to follow our own path, regardless of how painful. I prefer to look at it from a spiritual perspective and, as such, I know that there has been a reason for whatever Pete has experienced and a bigger picture. And I believe that having gone through all that he has, Pete will have a greater understanding of himself and also the world. These are things that most other people never come to appreciate. I've always said that Pete is going to come back the biggest of all of us, because he has had to endure and survive such a long, deep dive into the valley of darkness. In his own way, Pete is a giant.*

Mike Clink: *With most of the bands that I work with there's always one person who makes a big impression on me and ends up being a life-long friend, not just a business relationship. That's who Pete is for me. To meet him is to fall in love with him. I love his sense of humour and* *he's vulnerable too. The persona that people see is sex, drugs and rock and roll, but there's more to him than that. There's a whole other side which is genuinely warm, funny and caring.*

He's also extremely talented. Whenever I do a session these days and mention that I'm working with Pete again, I'm still surprised at how many individuals have been influenced by him. Nikki Sixx told me the reason that he plays his particular style of Gibson bass is because of Pete; same thing with the bass player in Slash's band. Pete had a major impact on people, and not just stylistically but also entertainment-wise. People just want to emulate the guy.

We started work on his new record right after he had completed his treatment for cancer, so he was a little run-down and weak. As a result, it's taken us a long time to piece together, but Pete's is a story that doesn't simply come to an end. He sometimes doesn't like to talk about what's gone on in his past, but, good and bad, he knows that it's all part of his life. And right there, on this record, that's Pete's story, warts and all, and it's really, really good.

I'm sixty-five now, but still think like a seventeen-year-old, which I guess is one of the reasons I'm still alive. Cancer, of course, delayed my career, but music gave me something to focus my recovery on and a motivation. Just as I had when I kicked heroin, I knew that if I beat cancer I'd be able to stand tall and go out and perform again, and ultimately that gave me strength enough to pull through. Not that it's been easy. I still have these incredible bouts of tiredness and the pain in my stomach. I still have to fight off the urge to drink, too, but I've found weak beer or cider helps ease my various physical discomforts and the doctors have said it's OK for me to have a drop. I have to have a blood test every six months and the occasional scan, but the prognosis is good and, touch wood, will remain that way. I want to get fit so that I can tour once more. I actually went to the gym not long after finishing radiotherapy, but it was hellish. My nerve endings were still repairing, but I think it'll be all right for me to do that again now. And I've had to do an awful lot of practice. The first time I picked up a guitar after my recovery, I just couldn't get my fingers to work. And in any case, it's quite difficult to sit there and just plonk away on the bass, at least without something to back it up.

Eventually, though, I started to write again. And altogether, the songs that I've managed to get down in the past three or four years, they do tell my whole life story. My mum got to hear some of the earliest demos before she died. She would say to my brother, 'Neill, would you put Peter's tape on for me again, it really is very nice.' I thought that was a lovely way to describe a bunch of songs about heroin addiction and other stuff.

Writing for the album, I guess I've been compelled not just to look back at my life and me, but also to re-evaluate both. I've come to learn that I'm fragile at times, but then again also very tough. I've been able to take the knocks and falls. It was never my intention to hurt anyone and I've always strived to be a decent human being like Mum and Dad brought me up to be, but there are an awful lot of things I'd take back and fix if I could. I wouldn't have been divorced the number of times I have. I would have looked after money. I wouldn't have become a junkie and let people down because of being so messed up. And most of all, I regret the fact that Joanna and Bethina died, both through circumstances that could have been as a result of my influence.

Fatherhood was one of those things that I thought had been and gone for me, but my daughter Zowie got back in touch with me a few years ago now. Her husband, Kevin, is a good man and when Zowie decided she wanted to get to know me, he helped her to track me down. When we met up it was the first time I'd seen her since she was a very small child, but we bonded for sure. We've got very similar personalities, I think, and now spend quite a bit of time together. I can't make up for all the things I've missed, but it's a blessing to have Zowie in my life again.

It was much the same situation with Charlotte. For a long time, I was also estranged from her, because of how uncomfortable things were between her mother and me and also after she'd seen first-hand just how far gone on drugs I'd got. I let Charlotte down and hurt her just as much as Zowie, but we're also on speaking terms now and able to go out for a meal. I don't want either of them to feel that I would ever meddle in their lives, and there's still so much I don't know about them, but I'm grateful to at least have the chance to try and pick up some of the pieces with them. Zowie has three grown-up daughters and a son, and one of her daughters has children of her own. So I'm a great-grandfather now, which I don't care to admit.

I see my brother, Neill, more regularly than anyone else in the family. Dad and Mum dying within a couple of years of each other definitely drew us closer together. Neill's very successful; he works in insurance in the Gherkin Building in the City of London and has a home in France. Neill also hasn't been divorced, so has much more money than me. He was always interested in what I was up to and the music bug was in him as well, but we made different choices in life. That's why he's a high-flying executive now and I'm a former heroin addict who's written some good songs. The one consolation for me is that nowadays Neill looks five years older than I do. But then again, he doesn't colour his hair.

I'm a survivor, I guess, but it's not really much of a badge of honour to have pinned on you. I suppose because of my job I've ended up being a role model, and at times I have certainly revelled in the image of me as a rock-and-roll degenerate, but I never meant to inspire anyone else to go out and kill themselves with drugs. In general, though, I live a very quiet, normal life and I'm kind of all right. I do still need to be kept away from drugs and have to steel myself to take alcohol in moderation. If I use anything these days then it's cocaine, but that's very much once in a while and purely as a social thing if I'm offered. Bloody hell, I've bought up half of South America by now and that's more than enough for anyone. Rather than doing a line, these days I prefer to go for a long walk instead.

I've got to live my life in music, which is something you can't buy. I'd have still been slogging away at the Ministry of Defence otherwise, and there have been a hell of a lot of good times. It would be fair to say that I've left a trail of destruction behind me, but that was the rock-and-roll lifestyle of the time: you wrote songs, went out and played them, drank, did drugs and there was always another woman.

Good, bad or indifferent, I always gave my best in the studio and onstage. And at my best, with UFO and alongside Phil, Michael, Paul and Andy, we were able to have a positive effect on people's lives and one that's endured. The fans, I think, liked the fact that there was a guy in the band who'd fall on his back on stage and spit out Jack Daniel's. The version of the band that's carried on and is still out there now might be more regimented, but there's a certain feel that I bring to the party which is lacking. They were a proper rock-and-roll band with me in it.

I'm sure plenty of people would like to see another reunion of the line-up that made *Strangers in the Night*, but for me now it would be like taking a step back. There are only so many times you can talk to people about *Doctor Doctor*. I do miss the guys, though. Through so many of the ups and downs in my life I had the band, my team, but now it's just me. The thing is, though, you can't simply recreate something, because the best music happens as if by magic and on pure instinct. And the greatest lesson I've come to learn is that neither of those things come out of a bottle or a packet.

———

Mike Clink: I think Pete feels that he has something to prove. UFO has continued to perform and make records, but he wasn't able to do that because of his substance abuse and then illness. It's not so much to the guys in UFO as to everybody that he wants to show he's still relevant and able to make music that people will love. Basically, he just wants to do what he loves most in the world, which is to get out on the road, in front of people and play for them.

It's been very different working with him this time, but only because he now has to be the frontman and we've done a bunch of stuff remotely. But he is still able to make me laugh like no one else. And the songs that he writes are genuinely heartfelt: Pete's not afraid to wear his feelings on his sleeve.

Jenny Way: Pete's been through so many hard times, my God he has, and at times he's almost given up, which was very sad to see. But he lives to perform and perhaps that's why I love him so. He needs to have an audience, but he's also a damn good songwriter and so dedicated to his craft. And he can still deliver, but he's not getting any younger. I just desperately want to see him have one last shot at the spotlight. He's worked so very hard to get himself back on track and he deserves that at least.

I decided to call the new album *Walking on the Edge*, because that's as good a way as any of summing up my life. It's been a wild, chaotic ride, truly it has. I've made a lot of friends, but I'm an erratic person. My love for music goes on, but sometimes drugs have got in the way of it. I wish I'd treated the women in my life better, but like to think that I've always had a good heart. I don't know what might be in store for me in the future, but I've got one more shot with rock and roll and intend to take it.

When I first sent the tape to Mike Clink, I never for a minute thought he'd want to make an album with me, but he did. From the start, Mike's believed in me. But he told me straight that he wanted to work with the real me, not the guy from out of a bottle, and I wasn't about to throw his faith in me away. It's taken us a long time to finish the record, with all sorts of obstacles along the way, but we've got some amazing people to play on it – guys like Slash, Nikki Sixx and Kenny Aronoff, one of the best session drummers in the world. That any of them would want to appear on my songs is beyond my wildest dreams. In the end, I've spent something like £50,000 of my own money on the album. I've flown to Los Angeles two, three times to do my parts, hired studios, paid for musicians, and now Jenny and I are having to scrape both barrels just to get by. But this is my last shot and I'm not going to pass it up. I've put my heart and soul into making this record the best that I can be, and would much rather use my money for something creative than stick it all in my veins.

Those albums UFO made in the 1970s, especially *Lights Out*, *Obsession* and *Strangers in the Night*, they're a formidable legacy, and even the band haven't matched up to them since. So I've got a lot to live up to. I hope on the back of *Walking on the Edge* that I can go back and do some of the places where I used to play with UFO. But the perfect thing that could happen would be if it allowed me to stop talking about the glories of the past and start living in the future.

It's been too long since I've been out on the road, though of course I do wonder what will happen once the bright lights are switched back on. But like I said, I'm tough, and determined not to be tempted back into the dark places I've been. I don't look, feel or act my age. I don't think about death any more, it's something that I'm happy to wait for. And people have bought into the legend of me doing this and that. Well, the last and best thing I want is for this legend to get back out there and be just as good as he's supposed to be.

ACKNOWLEDGEMENTS

I would like to thank my wonderful family, my brother Neill and his wife Sue. My late mother Ruth and father Fred who never stopped believing in me. My beautiful daughters to whom I owe more than they will ever know. Our manager Wilf Wright – the man who inspired UFO to play every club as if it was a stadium. The Schenker family – Michael for his friendship and Rudolph and their lovely mother for unstinting inspiration. All my colleagues from UFO and their families who would tell us we were good enough in the beginning even when we weren't. They instilled enthusiasm in us on so many occasions when we felt like giving up. Of course Andy and Phil who, without their friendship and chemistry, I wouldn't be writing this. All the journalists who were in our corner even when only twenty people would turn up to a gig especially Pete Makowski, Geoff Barton, Dave Ling, Garry Bushnell, Malcolm Dome, Dante Bonutto, Rich Davenport and others who know who they are. The evil photographer Ross Halfin, who was merciless in his quest for that elusive perfect shot, for his wicked sense of humour. To all that have sadly passed especially the much loved George Bodner and Randy Rhodes. John Knowles, the best tour manager of his time. My rock and roll friends who contributed to this book and those who helped corrupt me. There was only one Bon Scott. The genius Steve Harris – where would the world be without the mighty Maiden? Thanks to Ron Nevison for taking us to another level. To Mike Clink for all his kindness in recent years. To Ozzy and Sharon for their kindness and friendship – Ozzy, you are my hero. My friends Adam Davis and Chris La Marca and my right hand man Jason Poole. Super fan Dave Simpson and his lovely wife Elaine. All the staff at our record label Chrysalis who (nearly) always believed in us and Andreas Campomar and Claire Chesser at Little, Brown who are publishing this tome. To Paul Rees for his never-ending patience while I wrestled with my memory and Matthew Hamilton, my literary agent, for his help. Lastly I would like to thank my lovely wife Jenny for having such a beautiful soul and staunch love for me and providing support in all areas of my life.

Pete Way